CREATIVE CAREERS
FILM

D0589045

SFACTORY

Milly Jenkins

trotman

Creative Careers: Film
This first edition published in 2003 by Trotman and Company Ltd
2 The Green, Richmond, Surrey TW9 1PL

© Trotman and Company Limited 2003

Produced in association with Channel 4 **IDEAS**FACTORY

Editorial and Publishing Team
Author Milly Jenkins
Editorial Mina Patria, Editorial Director; Rachel Lockhart, Commissioning
Editor; Anya Wilson, Editor; Erin Milliken, Editorial Assistant
Production Ken Ruskin, Head of Pre-press and Production
Sales and Marketing Deborah Jones, Head of Sales and Marketing
Managing Director Toby Trotman

Designed by XAB

British Library Cataloguing in Publication Data
A catalogue record for this book is available from the British Library

ISBN 0 85660 903 X

Typeset by Mac Style Ltd, Scarborough, N. Yorkshire
Printed and bound in Great Britain by The Cromwell Press,
Trowbridge, Wiltshire

Contents

ABOUT THE AUTHOR

Milly Jenkins studied history at Manchester University and then broadcast journalism at Cardiff University. She started her career as a researcher for BBC Radio Wales, going on to work on news and current affairs documentaries for BBC Radios 4 and 5.

She has also worked as a writer and editor at the *Guardian* and is now a freelance journalist, specialising in careers and working life. She has written for the *Independent*, *The Times*, the *Financial Times*, the *Evening Standard* and *Marie Claire*. She lives in London.

ACKNOWLEDGEMENTS

Thanks to Helen Boyes at Skillset, Mark Batey at the Film Distributors' Association, John Innes at *Sight & Sound*, Dominic Eames at FilmFour.com, Nic Wistreich at Shooting People, Ben Craig at Filmmaking.net, and Redbus Film.

Also, to Adam Gee, James Estill, Julian Mobbs and Katie Streten at Channel 4's **IDEAS**FACTORY and to Mina Patria, Anya Wilson and Rachel Lockhart at Trotman.

Most of all, a big thank you to all the people who work in film who agreed to be interviewed for this book.

'If you make it – if you can get the right training and your foot on the first rung of the ladder – you're in for a good time. You will meet hundreds of people and go to a hundred different places.'

what this book will do for you

Well, so do a lot of people. Film is a tough, competitive business. It is estimated that 60,000 new people try to break into the audio-visual industries in the UK – TV, radio, film and interactive media – every year. That's a lot, considering 200,000 already work in them.[1]

More bad news. The number of people working on films, especially feature films, is tiny. Every year Skillset, an organisation that monitors and develops skills in the audio-visual industries, does a census to see how many people are working on any given day. In 2002, it found just 1,500 people working on film productions on the day it did its survey.

The *good* news is that working in film doesn't just mean working on feature films. Thousands more people work on films, drama series and documentaries for TV, on commercials and corporate productions, as well as for animation, visual effects and post-production companies. All in all, about 50,000 people work in the film and video industries.[2]

Even so, getting into film is hard. It takes talent and determination. And that's why it's important to find out exactly what a career in film involves and what you need to make it *before* you set out.

More good news. If you do make it – if you can get the right training and your foot on the first rung of the ladder – you're in for a good time. You will meet hundreds of people and go to a hundred different places. It's hard work and there is very little stability, but that's partly why the people who love it do it.

> **❝❝** INSIDERS TELL IT LIKE IT REALLY IS
>
> 'It's a great industry. The things I've seen and done I wouldn't swap for the world.'
>
> *Becky, Sound Recordist and Boom Operator*
>
> 'I don't think I've ever done a production that I haven't enjoyed, although looking back I probably did some moaning at the time. The hours are long and unsociable, the pay is not good and, as a runner, you're at the bottom of the pile. But it's great to be part of something creative. People always stress that it's not glamorous, and it isn't – but whenever I've done something high profile, working on a big set and meeting famous actors, and then seeing it on the screen, I can't help but love it.'
>
> *Josh, Runner*
>
> 'Would I recommend a career in film? Absolutely. It's a really exciting and innovative industry to work in. You get to meet and work with a wide range of people and get to work in amazing places and countries. The social side is fantastic. But it's also incredibly competitive and there is little long-term stability. You need to go in with very clear expectations, be hard-working, humble and persistent. It is much harder to break into than other industries.'
>
> *Helen Boyes, Film Co-ordinator, Skillset*
>
> 'I enjoy working, when I'm working. Every day is different. You never stop learning and there are always challenges along the way. But you

NEVER get paid enough money and when I'm not working I get miserable and wish I did something else.'

Phil, Art Department Assistant

'You do some great travelling, and when you're working on exciting projects with an exciting script, that you think is going to be the next big thing, it's the best. But when you're working long hours, on low pay, on a crappy project, you can feel very fed up.'

Laura, Production Assistant

WHAT THIS BOOK WILL DO FOR YOU

This book is a guide to working in film. It will tell you about the state of the film industry, where it has got to and where it is going. It will tell you what it's like to work in film on a day-to-day basis: what the working environment is like, what the people are like and what the money is like.

It will also explain who does what in film, helping you explore the kind of jobs you might be suited to, as well as telling you how to train for them and then find work in them. You'll hear from people already in those jobs, talking about how they got into the industry and what they love and hate about their work.

Like the rest of the Creative Careers series on working in the media – in television, film and radio – the aim is to give you the real deal on what it's like to work in film, highlighting some hard realities as well as some positives about a career in what can be a very challenging and rewarding business.

A STYLE NOTE
Throughout this book, the word 'film' is used in its most general sense, to mean feature films, short films, dramas, documentaries, animation, commercials, pop 'promos', and corporate non-broadcast films. For the sake of easy reading, 'film' is used as shorthand for the whole film-making industry.

ON THE WEB

The **IDEAS**FACTORY website (www.channel4.com/ideasfactory; www.ideasfactory.com/film_tv/index.htm) offers an invaluable resource to young creatives looking to get in and get on in the UK's Film industry. It provides a wealth of inspiration and information in the form of fresh, challenging, original features, games, masterclasses, etc. Plus careers, business, training and funding information and services, as well as region-specific 'hubs'. **IDEAS**FACTORY users take advantage of the site's interactivity to create and post their personal profiles, small ads, and threads in the dynamic forums.

NOTES

1. *Skills for Tomorrow's Media*: The Report of the Skillset/DCMS Audio Visual Industries Training Group, September 2001.
2. Office for National Statistics *Labour Force Survey*, Autumn 2002.

'The 1990s were boom times for British film. The number of films made by British companies rocketed, and so did the number of people going to the cinema.'

the past, the present, the future

THE PAST

The 1990s were boom times for British film. The number of films made by British companies rocketed, and so did the number of people going to the cinema. In 1996, there were an amazing 128 feature films produced here, compared to just 41 back in 1986. In the same time, the number of cinema tickets sold every year almost doubled.

Films such as *Four Weddings and a Funeral* helped to kickstart a renaissance in British film, continued by box office hits such as *The Full Monty*, *Notting Hill*, *Bean*, and *Lock, Stock and Two Smoking Barrels*. The film industry was also given a major cash injection by the National Lottery, as well as a big boost from the introduction of enhanced tax relief for film makers.

Suddenly there was funding for British films and strong incentives for American producers not only to invest in films here, but also to make their own ones here too. With tax breaks, cost-effective filming locations and a highly skilled workforce, Britain was a great place to be for film makers.

ON THE WEB

Loads of films get made in Britain. To find out exactly where, take a look at Movie Map, a guide to some of the most popular film locations in the UK.

(*See Movie Map at* www.visitbritain.com/movie map.)

THE PRESENT

Since the turn of the century, things have slowed down. Cinema admissions continue to grow every year, as do the number of new cinemas, but fewer films are being made. In 2001, 96 films (many of them co-productions with other companies in other countries) were produced. A more ominous sign was that US investment in British films, studios and locations dropped by about two-thirds.

A common view is that things moved too fast in the late 1990s, that people got swept away in the excitement of the boom, and that good money was poured into not-so-good film projects: not enough care was put into developing strong scripts and making sure there were distributors willing to show the films in cinemas, or audiences willing to watch them. As a result, dozens of films got left on the shelf, gathering dust and never given a cinema viewing.

Cinema-going, then and now

Many more people are going to the cinema now than a few years ago, but cinema admissions are still nothing like they used to be. It all changed in the 1950s, when television came along. That said, the UK is still the third biggest cinema market in the world, behind America and Japan.

Cinema Admissions (millions)

1933	903
1943	1,541
1953	1,285
1963	357
1973	134
1983	66
1993	114
2002	177

(Source: Screen Digest/CAA/Neilsen EDI/Screen Finance)

means the outlook is grim for British film. The industry has always been on a roller-coaster ride, weathering the ups and downs of recessions, funding trends and world events. 'It's a very cyclical industry by nature,' says Helen Boyes, Film Co-ordinator at Skillset, the leading organisation for developing skills in the audio-visual industries. 'It's always impossible to say whether employment prospects are good for the future. You never know what's going to happen.'

There are some constants. Britain is widely acknowledged as having a strong, highly skilled film workforce. Even when business is slow, American and other international film-makers continue to come here to use our world-renowned studios, such as Pinewood and Shepperton, and our world-leading animation and visual effects professionals.

THE FUTURE

There are some signs of where things are heading. The film gold rush of the late 1990s has made everyone in the business more cautious, and many think that is a good thing. The emphasis now is not so much on funding and making small to medium-sized films, but on trying to create a viable film industry that makes big, commercially successful films that people will want to watch, not just here, but worldwide.

This is the stance being taken by the UK Film Council, the government body responsible for developing the industry. Instead of funding the production of new films, it is putting most of its money and energy into the business side, in particular into improving skills in script

Vital stat

The global market for film is estimated to be worth $60 billion a year, most of which is money made by US companies.

WHICH COUNTRY HAS THE LARGEST FILM INDUSTRY?

'If you mean largest in terms of film output, then India is by far the world's largest producer of cinema, with some 1,300 films made annually (although most of these are never screened outside the country). Reasonably close behind is the US with around 850 films. If, on the other hand, you mean which country exports the most cinema, then of course the US is a clear winner, with Hong Kong a surprisingly close second.'

(Source: Filmmaking.net at www.filmmaking.net)

> **"**
>
> 'When the Muses gave out talent cards, Britain got the biggest.'
>
> *Steven Spielberg, director of* Jaws, ET, Jurassic Park, Schindler's List, Saving Private Ryan *and more ...*
>
> 'As a nation we've got an uncanny ability to produce world-class filmmaking talents ... We've got superb writers, directors and actors ... We have outstanding studios and facilities companies, world-class costumiers, camera companies and digital post-production houses ... And we still have – just about – the finest technicians and craftspeople anywhere.'
>
> *Alan Parker, chairman of the UK Film Council and director of* Midnight Express, Fame, The Commitments, Evita *and more ...*
>
>

development, production accounting, marketing and distribution. It argues that unless Britain gets better at distribution, at selling and promoting home-made films abroad, the film industry will never grow.

In the future, there is likely to be a lot less talk about 'British films' and the 'British film industry'. Most films made here are already co-productions, made in association with studios and companies from other countries. Of the 96 films made in 2001, only 45 were home-grown, home-funded films, made by mostly British film workers. The Harry Potter films, and other big hits such as *Bridget Jones's Diary*, may be labelled 'British', but they are largely American.

Some people argue this is not a bad thing: we need to get away from old-fashioned notions of British film as a cottage industry, churning out small films about British 'issues'. Instead, we need to start thinking of ourselves as major, international players. It doesn't matter where the money comes from, the argument goes, just that we come up with creative ideas for big films that get made using our workforce.

'We are too parochial. On independent films it's very difficult to make more than £1m back from the UK market, meaning you have to get the rest from foreign territories and consistently we make films that do not sell well abroad. Most of our films lack universal appeal.'

Tim Bevan, co-founder of Working Title Films and producer of Bridget Jones's Diary, Captain Corelli's Mandolin, Billy Elliot, High Fidelity, Notting Hill, Elizabeth **and more ...**

(*Source: Channel 4's Making Movies* at www.channel4.com/film/makingmovies)

'We have to stop defining success by how well British films perform in Milton Keynes. This is a big world – really successful films like *Notting Hill* can make up to 85 per cent of their revenues outside the UK.'

Alan Parker, chairman of the UK Film Council and director of Midnight Express, Fame, The Commitments, Evita **and more ...**

It may also be that, in future, more films are made abroad, in cheaper locations in Asia and Eastern Europe. If so, British film workers need to get truly international in their outlook, and be willing to work wherever the industry takes them.

One thing is for sure. To thrive, here and abroad, the workforce is going to have to be a highly skilled one. British film workers already have a strong international reputation, but they are going to need to keep learning new

ON THE WEB

Project X is a website for film-makers who want to get digital. Check it out for information on where digital film making has got to and where it's going to. There is a film making guide for 'digital virgins' and a glossary to demystify all the digital jargon. (See www.elementalfilms.co.uk/projectx.)

skills. The fear is that as older workers, many of whom got a solid training with the BBC or the ITV networks, reach retirement, there could be sudden skills shortages.

There are far fewer formal training schemes than there used to be, and freelances are largely left to their own devices to find training. Skillset is working hard to reverse this trend, raising money from the industry to fund freelance training, but it is also going to be up to individuals to keep on their toes.

There has already been a big push towards 'multi-skilling', with people increasingly expected to be jacks-of-all-trades – Make-Up Artists now do hair as well as make-up, Assistant Editors work alone, instead of being helped by a second and third Assistant Editor. This multi-skilling trend is likely to continue, with everyone expected to move effortlessly between working with film, video or digital.

It is also hoped that new technology – digital cameras, new computer editing systems and advanced visual effects techniques – will help make film-making significantly cheaper. Instead of paying a fortune to develop film stock, film makers will be able to use state-of-the-art digital cameras. And instead of hiring hundreds of extras for a battle scene, film makers will be able to create them using visual effects.

In line with this new, slim-line, cost-conscious, commercially minded approach to film-making, there is little doubt that the workforce will need to be well-trained, multi-skilled and highly flexible.

'Almost everyone working in film production is freelance. That means self-employed. Very few people have staff jobs.'

the face of the workforce, the hours, the pay

So, what's it like working in film? Where are the jobs based and what are the hours like? How much work is there and who's most in demand? Does the film industry need more Directors or more Dolly Grips? How many women work in the business, and what does everyone earn? Read on ...

THE FREELANCE LIFE

Be warned – if you are looking to get your feet under a desk, in a nice secure job with a pension, this is not the business for you.

Almost everyone working in film production is freelance. That means self-employed. Very few people have staff jobs, and there are statistics to prove it: Skillset's Employment Census 2002 found a staggering 98 per cent of people in film production were self-employed.

Freelancing is a way of life throughout the audio-visual industries. Seventy per cent of people working in commercials are also freelance, for example. However, there are some areas that seem to offer a bit more stability, with staff jobs rather than short-term contracts as the norm: only 16 per cent of people in corporate production, 14 per cent of people in post-production and 10 per cent of people working in special effects are freelance.

The overwhelmingly freelance nature of film means that it is a risky business to go into. Even old pros, with years of experience under their belts, go for months without working. While the pay is not bad while you are in work (see The Money, page 20), pay packets have to be stretched to cover sometimes long periods of unemployment.

Apart from being shrewd with money, you also need to have the right temperament to survive freelance life. You need to be good at finding work and selling yourself – you can't wait around for people to call you. You also need to be able to weather the ups and downs, and not take it too personally when you don't get work.

However, there are many benefits of life as a freelance. You can pretty much choose when and where you work, and this freedom and flexibility can outweigh some of the harder aspects. For tips on how to tackle the freelance life, visit www.skillsformedia.com/getting_on/resources. Click on the advice section and you will find business advice, marketing tips and financial and legal information.

Jargon Buster

Pre-Production, Production and Post-Production
Films are made in three stages after the script has been finalised by the scriptwriter and editors:

Pre-Production – the planning stage. The Producer assembles a production team to organise the shoot. They hire a crew and equipment, find studios and locations to film in, work out a filming schedule and do everything else that needs to be done before filming begins.

Production – the filming stage. The Director, and the crew, shoot the film, ideally in as short a time as possible to keep spending down. At the end, the crew is disbanded.

Post-Production – the editing stage. The film is cut and fine-tuned by the Editor, Director, Producer and a post-production team. The sound (dialogue and music) are tinkered with and perfected, and any visual effects not caught on camera are added.

WHERE THE JOBS ARE

Another warning: nearly all the work in film is in London and the South East.

Forty-seven per cent of people working in the audio-visual industries in the UK are based in London, according to the Skillset Employment Census 2002. Another 15 per cent are outside London, in the South East. The next biggest employment area is the North West, with 9 per cent of the workforce, followed by Scotland with 6 per cent and the West Midlands with 5 per cent.

The London-centred nature of the film industry makes life hard for non-Londoners starting out in film. The capital is a tough city in which to turn up looking for work, with extortionate rents and high travel costs. People with a base in London, or parents or friends they can live with for a while, definitely have the advantage: they are in a much better position to take unpaid work experience or low-paid trainee jobs to get them started.

If you're not from London, and you really don't want to live there, don't despair. Loads of people working in film live all over the UK. Once you've established yourself, or even before then, there is no reason you can't live in the Outer Hebrides or the Scilly Isles. If you're working in production, on sets and locations, you'll be travelling all over the place anyway. It won't matter where you live – just that production companies who want to hire you know where to call you.

Also, you might want to work in a specialist area of film that has a strong base outside London. Animation, for example, has a capital of its own in Bristol. There are also specialist job markets in Gaelic, Irish and Welsh productions that could get you work in Scotland, Ireland or Wales.

That said, there are many jobs where the work is, and will probably always be, predominantly based in London. If you want to be an editor, for example, most of the facilities houses are in London, mostly in Soho, and it's not (yet) work you can do anywhere from home – you usually need to be there, in person, in the editing suite.

JARGON BUSTER

Facilities House
A facilities house is a company that hires filming equipment and editing space. They can help with all aspects of post-production, supplying editors and/or editing suites where directors can take their film, edit it, and do the sound, voice-overs, graphics and effects.

THE FACE OF THE WORKFORCE

So what does the film workforce look like? Well, it's fairly, but not overwhelmingly, male. It's also quite white and there aren't many workers with disabilities. Nor are there a lot of grey heads – the biggest working age group is the 26–35 one, although the average age of freelances is 39, according to the Skillset Freelance Survey 2000–1.

WOMEN
Film has traditionally been a male-dominated business. Less so now. Overall, across the UK's audio-visual industries, 39 per cent of the workforce is female, according to the Skillset Employment Census 2002.

This is a smaller proportion than in the rest of the UK workforce, where women account for 46 per cent of all workers. Women are on much more of an equal footing with men in TV, commercials and radio, where they mostly make up nearly 50 per cent of the workforce, than they are in film. Just 15 per cent of people working in film production are women.

Women also still tend to do 'women's' work. Ninety-three per cent of Make-Up and Hair Artists are female, as are 82 per cent of people working in Costume and Wardrobe. Yet only 8 per cent of lighting operatives,10 per cent of camera workers and 11 per cent of sound experts are women.

Don't let any of this put you off, if you are female and want to work in cameras, lighting, sound or any other supposedly 'male' domain. The people recruiting for training schemes are more than aware of these inequalities and are, hopefully, trying to address them. If you can get the right training, get your foot in the first door and put up with the odd bit of laddishness on set, there'll be nothing to stop you smashing the 'celluloid ceiling'.

Another thing to bear in mind before embarking on a career in film is whether you think you can combine film work with having kids, should you want them. Forty-two per cent of women working in the audio-visual industries are freelance. In theory, that should make life easier for them, giving them some flexibility. In practice, many women who work on sets struggle: juggling children with 12-hour days, often a long way from home, is tough.

ETHNIC MINORITIES
Not nearly enough people from ethnic minorities work in film. Throughout the audio-visual industries, ethnic minorities make up 8.2 per cent of the

workforce, according to the Skillset Employment Census 2002. This was an improvement on previous years.
However, this headline figure is misleading. When you consider that most work is based in London, where ethnic minorities make up a quarter of the working population, you realise how underrepresented they are. Also, a closer look at the figures reveals that the biggest employment area for ethnic minorities is in cinemas, as cleaners, box office and kiosk staff.

Ethnic minorities account for much more of the workforce in TV (8 per cent) and radio (8 per cent), than in film production (1 per cent) and commercials (0.1 per cent). In animation, corporate production and post-production they make up 3–4 per cent of the working population. In terms of specific jobs, 5.6 per cent of producers, 6.5 per cent of production staff, 3.4 per cent of art department staff, 5 per cent of camera workers and 5.8 per cent of runners are from ethnic minority backgrounds.

PEOPLE WITH DISABILITIES

Only 0.8 per cent of employees in the audio-visual workforce have disabilities, compared to 12 per cent of the UK workforce as a whole. In addition, 0.8 per cent of freelances have disabilities. A close look reveals that people with disabilities are better represented in TV, radio and interactive media, than they are in film production and commercials.

Why is this so? In 2002, the UK Film Council did some research into the issue. It found access was still a major problem in training and that production budgets rarely allowed for reasonable adjustments to enable people with disabilities to work. 'Some view the film

---

Vital stat
Women directed just 10 of the 118 films produced in Britain in 2002.

(Source: British Council)

ON THE WEB

Black Filmmaker Magazine comes out six times a year, with news and features about black filmmakers in the UK and worldwide. Read it online at www.blackfilmmakermag.com

industry as employing "workers who can work successfully in very poor conditions, including working very long hours without their personal needs requiring any consideration whatsoever"', said the research.

All in all, they were depressing findings. The UK Film Council has suggested that the only way to improve work opportunities for people with disabilities would be to introduce quotas and targets. It is also planning to make awareness of disability issues a condition of funding.

WHO'S IN DEMAND?

Ask any classroom full of film and media students what it is they want to do in film, and most of them will say the same thing – they want to direct.

Very few of them will. Lots of people start out thinking they want to direct and, on their way, discover there are hundreds of other equally interesting, highly skilled, challenging jobs in film. To get a taste of some of them, and to learn what it is they actually entail, see Chapter 4.

If it really is your burning, dying ambition to direct, don't be easily put off, whatever this book or anyone else says. If you think you've got what it takes to be the next George Lucas, Mike Leigh or Guy Ritchie, grab a camera and get making your first short film. See Doing it For Yourself (page 82).

If not, keep a close eye on where the skills shortages are in film, and try to be one of the people who gets to fill them. These are the broad areas in the audio-visual industries with skills gaps, identified by the Department for Culture, Media and Sport:

- Sales
- Marketing
- Administration
- Accountancy
- Financial Planning.

Directing, you'll note, is not in there. More specifically, the Film Policy Review Group, a government body that wrote a major report on the film industry back in the late 1990s, said the industry needed more:

- Production Accountants
- Line Producers

- Script Readers and Editors
- Craft and Technical Grades – Carpenters, Plasterers, Electricians, Camera and Lighting experts, etc.

Both these lists reflect what the UK Film Council has been saying – the industry needs more business-minded people, working in production accounting and in distribution, as well as creative people working in script development, nurturing and perfecting scripts that will make great films.

Jargon buster

Distribution
Distribution companies, aka Distributors, buy films from production companies and sell them to cinemas, or 'exhibitors' as they're called in the industry. They also sell them to television channels. They advertise and promote the film, trying to get as many people to see it in as many cinemas as possible.

It also needs a new generation of highly skilled craft workers and technicians. At the moment, not enough people are getting the specialised training they need, but those that do won't be short of work. Plasterers, carpenters and electricians, for example, are already in high demand, and often able to name their price for work.

> **"**
>
> 'As proud as we are of our existing talent and skills base, there simply aren't enough good new writers, new editors, new production designers and new cinematographers coming through. The technical and skills workforce is ageing ... We desperately need a new generation of talented filmmakers because they are our life-force and our future.'
>
> *Alan Parker, chairman of the UK Film Council and director of* Midnight Express, Fame, The Commitments, Evita *amongst others ...*
>
> 'There are many jobs which people rarely think of – the industry needs electrical engineers, carpenters, plasterers, IT specialists and managers probably more than it needs producers, directors or camera people. If you want work in film and television simply because you want to do something "creative", ask yourself what you really mean by that.'
>
> *PACT, the Producers Alliance for Cinema and Television*
> (*Source: PACT at* www.pact.co.uk)
>
> **"**

THE WORKPLACE

Forget any notion you might have of cool, advertising agency-style offices, long leisurely lunches and a 9–5 day. Working in film is hard work, in often terrible working conditions.

If you work in a production office, chances are you'll be working in a cramped and pokey space with ancient facilities and a serious shortage of desks. When filming begins, it gets worse – part of the production team may move to a makeshift office in a Portakabin near the set.

The key to survival is the ability to make do with whatever space and facilities you have. If you need to get 50 scripts copied in a hurry, the photocopier is broken and you're in the middle of nowhere, you will have to use your initiative. Moaning about it will not go down well.

If you work on the set itself, working life will be even less comfy. The hours are very, very long. Getting up at 5am is common. Twelve hours is good going for a day's shoot, but 16 hours or more are by no means unusual. If you decide you've had enough and go home at 6pm, you'll never get a job again.

It can be also be incredibly cold, if you're outside, not to mention tiring, standing around for hours and hours on end. Lots of jobs require you to be there the whole time, with maybe just a few breaks for lunch and tea. (One big perk is the food – massive feasts served up from a catering bus.) Film workers say it takes a long time to build up the physical and mental stamina you need to work like that, six days a week, week in week out.

If you think you can't hack those kind of hours and conditions, you could get a job that never requires you to be on set. But even then, you're unlikely to find a stable, 9–5 job. Even in offices and facilities houses there are going to be times when there is a big rush on, requiring all-nighters and weekend work. And the working conditions still won't be a delight – if you want to be an editor, for example, you are going to be in dark, windowless editing suites for hours on end.

Aside from the working conditions, a career in film can be tough for other reasons too. Although everyone dresses casually, and it may at first glance look like a young, relaxed working culture, film is surprisingly strict and hierarchical. Everyone starts at the bottom and works their way up. You're expected to know your position in the pecking order, and stick to it: getting above your station is frowned on. People in senior positions have no qualms about shouting at people in junior roles.

That's the downside. The upside is that there can be great camaraderie. Because the work is so intensive, you get to know people really well and often meet up with them again in future jobs. Friends recruit and recommend friends, so once you've made some you can find yourself working with people you really like on every job.

My experience

'An average day at work is long. Filming days are usually a minimum of ten hours, and pop promos usually last 18 hours. The working environment is very intense and tensions can run high as there is always a lot of time pressure to fit all the shots in. This can make it an exciting atmosphere to work in and you rely on adrenaline to keep going. Having said this, some days can be relatively calm and there can be some shoots with long stretches of time waiting around. Physically it is very demanding and the working environment in large studios is pretty grim – large black airless spaces.'

Kate, Clapper Loader

'You work incredibly hard when you're working, often six days a week for three months. At the end of a film you're exhausted. Lots of people get ill from exhaustion. When a job is over, instead of relaxing for a while, you're immediately worried about where the next job is going to come from. It's a very extreme freelance life.'

Laura, Production Assistant

THE MONEY

Working in film (probably) won't make you rich, and at first you'll (definitely) be quite poor. If you get to a senior job, you'll be well paid. But the freelance nature of the film business means very few people get an annual salary, and therefore regular pay cheques. Anything you earn has got to cover you while you're working *and* all the periods when you're not in work.

Given how few features get made, almost everyone works across the industry, in features when they can, but also in TV and on commercials and 'non-broadcast' corporate productions. Loads of big name film-makers do ads – it's where the money is, and it helps fund the significant amount of unpaid time they spend planning and developing features.

'It can be really horrible how some people speak to you. You can also be totally ignored. The attitude is: "Everyone's been in that crap job. I was and got treated badly, so you can be too." In some ways it helps to know that the Producer had to do the same lowly jobs. It seems fair. Other times, it feels like a ridiculously old-fashioned fagging system.'

Karen, Runner

'It is a very small world. Some people love that, others find it claustrophobic. If you fall out with someone more senior than you, or do a bad job, word goes round very fast. Unless you've got an exceptional skill, you're a talented technician, it's very hard to get your reputation back and to find work again.'

Sarah, Casting Assistant

'Film takes over your life. It looks tremendously exciting, but when you get into your 30s, it's hard to juggle work and your life outside it. It's very hard to integrate your working life with your friends' and family's lives. You disappear for six weeks at a time and life goes on without you. Women with children have a hard time. As a result, there are a lot of unhappy and frustrated people in the industry. No one believes that when they're starting out – I didn't.'

Becky, Sound Recordist and Boom Operator

EARNING CURVE

Because film professionals are mostly freelance, it's hard to get a picture of what people, on average, earn every year. It depends how much work they get and how well the industry is doing at the time. It can be feast *or* famine.

To give you a rough idea of what the money is like, here are the minimum rates in the Freelance Production Agreement, agreed by BECTU, the Broadcasting, Entertainment, Cinematograph and Theatre Union, and PACT, the Producers Alliance for Cinema and Television. Remember though, these are weekly rates and very few people are in work every week of the year. Also, bear in mind that people haggle a lot in this business, so rates vary dramatically, depending on the individual's experience and the kind of work they're being offered.

If you work on a set, chances are you'll be working 12 hours a day, six days a week – that's 72 hours a week. The BECTU rates vary depending on how many hours a week you're working, so this earnings chart shows you what you get for a 40-hour week *and* a 72-hour week. There is a separate agreement for the commercials sector – to see it, check out the BECTU website (www.bectu.org.uk/resources/agree).

Weekly rates	40-hour week	72-hour week
Art Department Assistant, Technical Assistant	£251	£552
Production Secretary, Third Assistant Director	£281	£618
Clapper Loader, Junior Make-Up/ Hair Assistant, Publicity Assistant	£375	£825
Sound Assistant, Graphic Artist, Assistant Script Supervisor	£389	£855
Wardrobe Assistant, Props Person, Assistant Editor	£430	£946
Dubbing Editor, Production Co-ordinator, Third Assistant Director	£455	£1,000
Boom Operator, Location Manager, Focus Puller, Grip	£496	£1,092
Production Buyer, Set Decorator, Unit Publicist	£528	£1,160
Camera Operator, Art Director, Editor, Production Accountant	£570	£1,254
Construction Manager, Costume	£644	£1,417
Designer, Chief Make-Up/Hair Director, Director of Photography, Producer, SFX Supervisor	*Individual negotiation*	

(Source: BECTU and PACT Freelance Production Agreement, January 2001)

" MY EXPERIENCE – THE MONEY

'You negotiate your pay with every job. It's a bit like you're a car being hired. They call lots of people, ask what their rates are and then negotiate with you, depending on the number of days of work there are. Pay per day for my job is between £180 to £250, but it varies around the country. You get paid most in London. That may look like good pay, but multiplied by the number of days you work a year, and it's not necessarily so good. You might only get 100 days work, or if you're lucky 200. Also, we're talking 12-hour days, so the hourly rate isn't actually that good.'

Becky, Sound Recordist and Boom Operator

'It's common not to get work for six months. Lots of people work in commercials or different fields, others rely on bank loans and credit cards to see them through ... When you're starting out you need to be flexible about money. You'll be negotiating pay throughout your career, but you need to be particularly flexible at first.'

Helen Boyes, Film Co-ordinator, Skillset

'My commercial rate of pay for a ten-hour day is £270, and after that I get overtime, so I think the pay is very good. I love the money and the freedom it gives me – as I don't have to work full-time I can really use my spare time to pursue other interests'.

Kate, Clapper Loader

'I had one job where I was being paid £75 a week. One day the director gave me £200 in cash and asked me to go out and get him a lobster platter for lunch from somewhere in Soho. That was kind of irritating.'

Karen, Runner

"

'What, exactly, is a Best Boy or a Key Grip? What does a Gaffer do?'

4. THE JOBS

what are the skills you need to make it?

WHAT IT TAKES

Before we take a look at exactly who does what in film, it's worth having a think about what skills you need to make it in the industry.

As you'll see, the jobs are very diverse – the skills you need to be a good Camera Operator are not necessarily the same as the ones you need to be a successful Producer. That said, there are some universal skills that *everyone* working in film needs to have. You will need to be all of the following if you want to get ahead...

TEN THINGS THEY'LL LOVE ABOUT YOU
1. Creative
2. Independent
3. Self-starting
4. Flexible
5. A good talker
6. ... and an even better listener
7. Able to take orders
8. Reliable and hardworking

9. A lateral-thinking problem solver
10. A diplomatic team worker.

THE CREW

It takes hundreds of people to make a feature film. The sheer number of people involved, not to mention their sometimes bizarre-sounding job titles, is mind-boggling. What, exactly, is a Best Boy or a Key Grip? What does a Gaffer do? To show you just how many different jobs there are on a big production, here's what the full credits on a recent British hit, *Bend it Like Beckham*, looked like:

Director	FT2 Trainee
Producers (2)	Art Director
Scriptwriters (3)	Set Decorator
Executive Producers (5)	Standby Art Director
Director of Photography	Assistant Art Director
Line Producer	Art Department Consultant
Editor	Graphic Designer
Production Designer	Assistant Props Buyer
Costume Designer	Art Department Assistant
Hair and Make Up	Junior Buyer
Original Score Composer	Property Master
Music Producer	Driver/Storeman
Music Supervisor	Dressing Props
Casting Directors (2)	Standby Props
Second Unit Director	Additional Standby Props (3)
Production Manager	Camera/Steadicam Operator
First Assistant Director	Additional Camera Operators (4)
Second Assistant Director	Focus Puller
Third Assistant Director	Additional Focus Pullers (6)
Additional Third Assistant Director	Clapper Loader
Floor Runners (2)	Camera Trainees (3)
Runner/Drivers (2)	Camera Truck Driver
Production Co-ordinator	Still Photographer
Assistant Production Co-ordinator	Stills Assistant
Production Secretary	Gaffer
Production Assistant	Best Boy
Production Runners (2)	Electricians (2)
Football Coach and Co-ordinator	Grip
Script Supervisor	Additional Grips (5)

Genny Op

Driver

Production Sound Mixer

Boom Operator

Second Boom Operator

Costume Supervisor

Costume Assistant

Costume Trainee

Make Up and Hair Artists (2)

Daily Make Up and Hair Artists (2)

Make Up and Hair Assistant

Make Up Trainee

Henna and Nail Art

Unit Publicity

Asian Press

Production Accountant

Assistant Accountant

Post Production Accountants (2)

Associate Producer

Post Production Supervisor

Assistant Editor

Post Production Assistant

Visual Effects Supervisor

Lead Digital Artist

Digital Artists (3)

Timer

Supervising Sound Editor

ADR Supervisor

Dialogue Editors (2)

Sound FX Editors (2)

Re-recording Mixers (2)

Digital Assistant

ADR Mixers (2)

ADR Recordists (2)

ADR Casting

Stage Recordist

Foley Editor

Foley Mixer

Foley Artists (2)

Foley Assistant

Location Manager

Additional Location Manager

Locations Assistant

Scout

Construction

Construction Manager

Charge Hand Carpenter

Carpenters (4)

Stage Hand

Scenic Artist

Lead Painter

Painters (2)

Construction Buyer

Standby Rigger

Nurse

Unit Drivers (2)

Production Bus Driver

American Trailer Driver

Chef

Assistant Chefs (2)

Dining Bus Driver

Lawyers (2)

Music Consultant

German Unit (20)

Road Movies Team (9)

THE BIG JOBS

So what do all these people do? Let's look at some of the big jobs first –
Director, Producer, Scriptwriter, Director of Photography, Editor,
Production Designer and Costume Designer – taking it from the top with
the supremo of the set. Have a look at How They Got There, on page 48,
which will give you an idea of where you should be starting if you're setting

your sights on being a Director or any of the other 'big jobs'.

DIRECTOR

The Director takes the script from the page to the screen. They are responsible for the creative vision of the film. Usually hired by a producer, unless they are producing the film themselves, the Director conveys their vision of the script to their key staff: the Director of Photography, the Production Designer and the Costume Designer – it is their job to make the Director's vision come to life. The Director helps cast the film, decide on locations and plan the shoot. They sometimes write, or rewrite, the script. When filming begins, they have total creative control of the set, giving directions to the cast and the camera crew. Afterwards, they work closely with the Editor, cutting and fine-tuning the film.

PRODUCER

The Producer is a creator, entrepreneur and manager rolled into one. They oversee the film from beginning to end – from the initial concept right through to distribution and publicity. It is often the Producer who develops the original idea, buying the rights to the book or play, if it's an adaptation, commissioning a Scriptwriter and finding a Director. Some Producers work on the script itself, writing and editing it. Others stick to the business side – the tricky task of raising the finance for the film and then bringing it in, within budget. The Producer hires the crew, manages the entire filming and editing process and then has to find a distributor to show it in cinemas. It is up to the Producer to get the maximum possible profit out of the film so that investors get their money back. All in all, it is a massive job.

SCRIPTWRITER

The Scriptwriter, aka Screenwriter, obviously, writes scripts. Sometimes that means coming up with an original story idea, writing a treatment or a script, and then selling it to a Producer. Alternatively, they might get commissioned to write up someone else's idea, or to adapt a book or play into a screen play. Established Scriptwriters have agents who find them

INSIDER TIPS

'You need very particular personal qualities – stamina, perseverance, humility, flexibility. Working 16 hours a day with a team in a small room – that's when those personal qualities come into play.'

**Helen Boyes, Film
Co-ordinator, Skillset**

'This has to be the thing you most want to do, because if you don't have that absolute drive and commitment, someone else will. Nothing is handed to you.'

**Becky, Sound Recordist and
Boom Operator**

On the job

'Being a director is not an easy job. The director is the main link between the creative and the technical teams, communicating artistic and practical content. They carry a great amount of responsibility on the project's success. They need to adapt to every new situation, learn the latest technology and find their place in the competitive world of media.'

(*Source: The Directors Guild of Great Britain,*
www.directorstraining.org.uk)

My experience

'Being on the shoot is actually my favourite part of the process, but I don't know if I appreciate it at the time! You can see the end result and think it's great, but when I'm there on the shoot and directing it, I quite enjoy the pressure of getting that script off the page in a way that's both accessible and enjoyable ... although I do often come off a shoot tearing my hair out.'

Rebecca Hardy, independent film-maker
(*Source:* **IDEAS**FACTORY *at* www.channel4.com/ideasfactory)

What it takes

'The Director, in the true sense of the word, is someone who can shape a vision and has something to say, not just someone who likes creating a glittering surface with lots of groovy shots. A proper Director

" ON THE JOB

'The role of the producer is all-encompassing. It's the most important and the most invisible. You are the first in and the last out, in terms of involvement. For instance on *East is East*, I identified the project, I saw a play, fell in love with it, I set about getting the rights, persuaded the writer and his agent that I was the right person to produce this film, then worked on it with the writer and developed it, turning it from a play into a feature film. Then I had to raise the money; that in itself was a mega-battle of several months. Having raised the money, I then had to choose the team. So I hired the is someone with a voice, not just one of the thousands of people who are quite good at imitating what they've already seen on TV.'

Pawel Pawlikowski, documentary maker and feature writer-director, including Last Resort

Directors' top directors

When *Sight & Sound* magazine asked well-known directors to name their all-time favourite films, these are the directors who came out tops:

1. Orson Welles
2. Federico Fellini
3. Akira Kurosawa
4. Francis Ford Coppola
5. Alfred Hitchcock
6. Stanley Kubrick
7. Billy Wilder
8. Ingmar Bergman
9. Martin Scorsese, David Lean and Jean Renoir

(*Source: Sight & Sound at* www.bfi.org.uk/sightandsound)

director, together with him assembled the crew and the heads of department, continued to work on the script, and then was solely responsible for delivering that film on time and on budget and of the highest possible quality. There is no pie that you haven't got a finger in, or indeed, for the most part have been responsible for baking! Of course if you go wrong, your house and goods are forfeit, so it's enormous pressure. But it is the most rewarding job imaginable.'

Leslee Udwin, Producer of East is East
(*Source: Channel 4's Making Movies at* www.channel4.com/film/makingmovies)

work and sell their ideas. Scripts are usually rewritten several times before going into production, and it is not uncommon for different writers to be brought in to work on different drafts – plenty of Scriptwriters make a living out of rewriting. When filming begins, Scriptwriters do not usually have much of a say in who gets cast and how their script is represented on screen, unless they have negotiated to have an Executive Producer role or have a close relationship with the Director and Producer.

ON THE JOB

'I love writing scripts. One of the things I love about it is that part of the art of it is trying to say a lot without using too many words. It's a very particular kind of writing, very sparse, more like writing poetry than prose. I also love the fact that the sky's the limit. You could write a script that makes you a multi-millionaire. Or, you could struggle all your working life to get anything made. It's definitely a job for dreamers. In terms of your day-to-day life, you're your own boss, you can work from home and organise your own time. If you're lucky, you do a mixture of working on your own and collaborating with others, going to meetings with Directors and Producers.'

Amy Jenkins, Screenwriter, including This Life *and* Elephant Juice

JARGON BUSTER

Treatment
A treatment is the scriptwriter's sales pitch – a summary, a few pages long, of the story and characters in the film they are proposing to write. It is written as a narrative, without dialogue, and needs to be punchy enough to grab the attention of the reader, hopefully a director or producer, and inspire them to commission a script.

On the web

Done Deal (www.scriptsales.com) is a classic website – it lists the latest scripts to get 'greenlighted' in Hollywood. Here are some pitches for films you can expect to see on the screen in future:

- *Paper Dragon* – A boy, who is a Rubik's Cube champ and computer whiz, is given an ancient Asian puzzle box. When he opens the box he finds a folded Chinese warrior inside that magically comes to life, and he and the warrior embark on adventure.
- *Silverfish* – A high-tech, high-stakes gambling ring arranges early prison releases for the fiercest of convicts. The ex-cons are then trained in martial arts weapons combat, transformed into modern-day gladiators and pitted against one another in arenas that turn the island of Manhattan into a modern-day Roman coliseum.

DIRECTOR OF PHOTOGRAPHY

The Director of Photography (DOP), aka the Cinematographer, creates the look and feel of the film. DOPs work closely with the Director and Production Designer, trying to turn their vision of the film into reality on screen. That means working with the lighting team to set up the lights for each shot and with the camera team, choosing the film stock and the

On the job

'Cinematography is a vital element in telling a film's story and keeping the audience interested in that story. While I believe that cinematography cannot save a flawed story idea, I do believe it has the possibility to enhance a good one.'

Neal Fredericks, Director of Photography on The Blair Witch Project (*Source: ReelMind at* www.reelmind.com)

camera angles, lenses and filters. On a small production, they sometimes double up as Camera Operator. Before filming begins, they help plan the shoot, agree on locations and work out what resources will be needed, and how much it is all going to cost.

Jargon Buster: *Film Stock*

The 'raw', unexposed film that is loaded into the camera for shooting. It can be colour or black-and-white, fast or slow.

EDITOR

Working together with the Director, the Editor cuts the film, choosing shots from each scene and putting the scenes in order to create a logical, smooth-running story – the final cut. Although it is a technical role, it can also be highly creative. Senior, well-respected Editors play as important a role as the Scriptwriter and Director in shaping the film – its structure and its look. It is not uncommon for films to undergo radical changes in the editing room. Film used to be cut manually, with 'rushes' from the film assembled on Steenbeck machines. Today rushes are usually transferred onto digital editing equipment.

My experience

'I consider it primarily creative. There are some people who think it's technical just because I do it on a computer … Most of the directors I work with will admit that a large part of my job is counselling because the directors come to me like they've come from a war zone, so I like to create a calm atmosphere.'

Jon Harris, Editor on Snatch
(*Source: IDEASFACTORY at* www.channel4.com/ideasfactory)

PRODUCTION DESIGNER

The Production Designer creates and designs the whole look of the film. They work closely with the Director to realise his or her vision. They also work closely with the Director of Photography and the Costume and Set Designers. They are responsible for the visual look of everything from the sets and locations to the art work and props. As head of the art department, they lead a large team of specialist staff and have to make sure everything is done within budget.

> ## My experience
>
> 'I love the diversity, the speed at which you have to come up with ideas and turn them around, the studio building and the final result.'
>
> **Alison Dominitz, Production Designer**

COSTUME DESIGNER

The Costume Designer creates all the costumes worn by the cast, working closely with the Director and Production Designer. After reading the script, they spend a significant amount of time on research before making the costumes a reality, either by making them from scratch or finding them elsewhere. They spend time with the actors, discussing their ideas and perception of the characters they are going to play. They may manage large Costume Departments.

> **❝** ON THE JOB
>
> 'The design process starts with research. What I do is get to know the script inside out, then start looking at hundreds of books to get a "feeling" for the character. I photocopy pictures and photographs and make a reference file for each character ... After I meet the actors I start thinking about which costumes will have to be made from scratch (this can cost up to £1,000) and which costumes I can make up by altering existing stock ... What the actors say is usually incredibly important ... There aren't many bad things about the job. The hours are long. It varies but I often have to get up at 5.30am to be on set in time to get the actors into costume so they can be on set for first light. You get a bit drained because the actors are naturally very demanding of you, they need you to give them your best.'
>
> *Phoebe de Gaye, Costume Designer*
> (*Source: Channel 4's Making Movies at*
> *www.channel4.com/film/makingmovies)*
>
> **❞**

ENTRY-LEVEL JOBS

What about the jobs at the other, bottom end of the ladder? Where did the people in the big jobs start out? Here are some of the entry-level jobs in film:

- Runner
- Production Assistant
- Clapper Loader/Camera Assistant
- Sound Assistant
- Lighting Assistant
- Assistant Location Manager
- Third Assistant Director
- Art Department Assistant

- Wardrobe Assistant
- Make-up/Hair Assistant
- Props Assistant
- Post Production Runner/Assistant Editor
- Casting Assistant.

RUNNER
A Runner ... runs around, fetching and carrying whatever they are asked to fetch and carry. There are different kinds of running jobs – Production Runners, aka Office Runners, who work in the production office, and Floor Runners, who work on set. Office runners may do administrative or organisational work, helping plan productions before and during filming. When filming starts, there may be several Floor Runners, each assigned to

---

" MY EXPERIENCE – BEING A RUNNER

'All Runners basically do whatever needs doing: helping carry props and equipment, rounding up crew and actors, driving to pick up supplies, lunches, equipment ... There are endless places on a film set where an extra pair of hands can be used for one reason or another. Runners are that extra pair of hands.'

Josh, Runner

'In production offices, the work can be pretty mundane – sticking labels on tapes, going to the post office. But you get to meet a lot of people, running around Soho doing errands. It can be very busy, and you get asked to do insane things. But there are quiet times too. When there isn't much work, you have to try and look busy. If you don't, you get asked to do stupid things, like rearrange the Coke cans in the cupboard. The great thing about office running jobs is that the hours are less insane than on a set.'

Karen, Runner

Vital stat

There are 1,300 Runners working in film and TV in the UK, according to Skillset. Forty-six per cent of them are freelance, 52 per cent are women and 5.8 per cent are ethnic minorities.

(*Source: Skillset Employment Census 2002*)

different departments (the art department, the camera crew, etc). If it's a small production, there may just be one runner, helping everyone out.

PRODUCTION ASSISTANT

The Production Assistant, aka the PA, helps the production team – the Producer, Line Producer, Production Manager and Production Co-ordinator – with anything administrative and organisational. The scope of the job depends on the scale of the film. In pre-production they help the Production Co-ordinator make booking arrangements and generally help plan the shoot. During filming, PAs usually help put together and circulate scripts, call sheets and daily reports. In post-production they might put together shot lists for the Editor or do any other necessary paperwork.

> ## MY EXPERIENCE – PRODUCTION ASSISTANT
>
> 'I do anything that needs sorting out in the production office, but I'm also the main point of contact for other departments, like art and sound, dealing with their problems and running errands for them. For example, lighting might call and ask me to fax through an order for them. I'm usually employed during pre-production and production.
>
> 'The great thing about this job is that you get to know everyone working in all the different departments, so you make a lot of contacts. The downside is that the hours are hellish – you're often first there and last home – and you work in some very pokey offices, often a make-shift Portakabin. Also, nearly all films overrun and you have to deal with angry agents and crew. You get a lot of stress and strain from the Producer and Director. But it's the best way to learn how films get made.'
>
> *Laura, Production Assistant*

CLAPPER LOADER

The Clapper Loader, aka Camera Assistant, is in charge of loading the film into the camera magazines and unloading the exposed film stock (or tapes if they're working with video). They label the exposed film and fill in forms, detailing what has been shot, preparing the film to be sent to the lab. As well as helping look after, and recharge, camera equipment, they help rig monitors and work the clapperboard, a visual and audio record of each shot – 'scene two, take one' – that later helps Editors in the cutting room put the pictures and sound in sync.

> **MY EXPERIENCE – CLAPPER LOADER**
>
> 'Every shoot is different and you have to think on your feet. Once we've set up the camera and I've loaded some initial film the pace is normally very fast and I'm running to catch up. Although clapper loading is essentially a pretty straightforward and repetitive job, I am rarely bored. I mainly work with the same camera crew so work often just feels like hanging out with good friends. I learn a lot as I'm always on set, near the action. You can learn a lot about directing. I hate the fact I can't leave the set for more than a few minutes in case the camera runs out of film. Sometimes the pressure is intense and I get really nervous about making a mistake and ruining some film.'
>
> *Kate, Clapper Loader*

SOUND ASSISTANT

The Sound Assistant assists the Sound Recordist and Boom Operator – the person who records the sound during filming and the person who holds the microphone. They may also be asked to do basic sound recording jobs, recording any background sounds or effects that are needed. A Sound Assistant may also work in post-production, helping Sound Editors and effects experts with their work. You won't always find a Sound Assistant in the credits – it depends how big a production it is.

LIGHTING ASSISTANT

The Lighting Assistant, when there is one, assists the lighting team – the Gaffer (the chief lighting technician), the Best Boy (the Gaffer's main assistant) and the electricians. They have usually already had some training as an electrician.

ASSISTANT LOCATION MANAGER

The Assistant Location Manager, aka the Location Assistant, does some of the leg work for the Location Manager – the person responsible for finding and organising locations for filming. They go out and about looking for suitable locations and then help organise permission and fees for filming there. Sometimes the Location Manager works alone, sometimes he or she has an Assistant, and sometimes there is another, more junior role, of Location Scout.

THIRD ASSISTANT DIRECTOR (3RD AD)

The 3rd AD usually works on set, making sure actors are dressed, made-up and on set in time for their scenes, organising extras and generally running around for the 1st AD, the 'foreman' of the set. They're one step down from 2nd ADs who mostly work in the production office, liaising between the set and the production team. Big productions have a 1st, 2nd and 3rd AD. On smaller ones, there is just an Assistant Director, who does the work of all three.

ART DEPARTMENT ASSISTANT

The Art Department Assistant, aka the Art Department Runner, helps out in the art department – the department responsible for sets, props and any

---

" MY EXPERIENCE – ART DEPARTMENT ASSISTANT

'I buy tea bags, milk, sugar – all that nonsense. But I also get to measure up and draw into plan form all the locations, make models, design graphics (logos, letters, signs for fictional establishments, etc). I also draw up details of sets for the construction team to build.'

Phil, Art Department Assistant **"**

art work. They can carry out basic tasks – running errands and ordering supplies. If they are lucky, they get to do more skilled work – period research, set drawings, prop making and set dressing.

WARDROBE ASSISTANT

The Wardrobe Assistant helps out in the Costume Department, aka Wardrobe, working for the Costume Designer and the Costume Supervisor, the person who runs the department on a day-to-day basis. Before filming, they may help create and/or find costumes. During filming they are on hand to clean and store costumes, and also to help dress actors and extras.

MAKE-UP/HAIR ASSISTANT

The Make-up and Hair Assistant - sometimes Junior Make Up and Hair Assistant – helps out in the make-up room, tidying up, ordering supplies and maybe doing extras' make-up and hair. They may also work on set, touching up actors' make-up and hair during filming.

PROPS ASSISTANT

The Props Assistant helps out in the props department of the art department, researching, finding, making and organising props, working for the Property Master/Mistress and any other prop staff.

POST-PRODUCTION RUNNER/ASSISTANT EDITOR

A Post-Production Runner is a Runner in a facilities house, running errands for editors, fetching film and tapes and helping organise the editing suite. On big films, the Editor may have several Assistant Editors – a 1st Assistant Editor, a 2nd Assistant Editor and maybe even a 3rd. Assistant Editors organise any material the Editor needs and keep records. It's up to them to make sure everything runs smoothly in the cutting room. If working with film, tasks include 'syncing up' the picture and sound rolls and ordering prints and reprints from the laboratory. If working with tape, they organise the tapes ready for editing. In a non-linear cutting room, that means digitising tape material on the computer, ready to be edited.

CASTING ASSISTANT

Casting Assistants work for Casting Directors, doing administrative and organisational work – making calls, sending faxes, opening letters, speaking to actors' agents and organising times for them to come in to do readings. They also do 'talent scouting' work for the Casting Director, going

> **❝ MY EXPERIENCE – CASTING ASSISTANT**
>
> 'Casting Directors don't run big offices. Often you're their receptionist, PA and Casting Assistant in one. Jobs can be permanent or temporary, when they have a big project on. It can be frustrating when Directors suddenly change their mind: you're told to find 50 people in their 50s with dark hair to audition and then the Director decides he want blondes in their 30s. The worst part of the job is dealing with so many disappointed actors who often don't get a job for totally random reasons.'
>
> *Sarah, Casting Assistant*
> ❞

to see new actors in drama school or theatre productions, reporting back on who might be worth auditioning.

OTHER JOBS ... IN A SENTENCE

Executive Producer – can be hands-on, raising finance and overseeing the producer, or an honorary title given as a perk to a financier, agent or actor.

Line Producer – a senior role, a producer with chief responsibility for all spending and logistical decisions on the set.

Production Manager – runs the production office, with responsibility for making sure the film is made on time and within budget, and that everyone has what they need to do their job.

Production Co-ordinator – often sets up the production office from scratch, overseeing the booking of crew, equipment and transport, and then, during filming, writing progress reports, call sheets and script revisions.

Production Accountant – manages the film's finances, working out budgets, keeping the books, sorting out the payroll and tax, overseeing cash flow and any other financial work required.

Casting Director – organises the casting process, working closely with the Director and Producer to secure the right actors for the right fee.

First Assistant Director – or 1st AD, the Director's right-hand person, breaks down the script into a filming schedule, manages the crew on set and pushes everyone to keep on schedule.

JARGON BUSTER

Continuity
Film scenes are shot out of sequence, not in the order they come in on the script. If a scene needs several takes, at different times and on different days, continuity needs to be maintained. That means making sure the actors are in exactly the same costumes, with the same make-up, camera positions, lighting and props.

Second Assistant Director – or 2nd AD, works with the production office, planning the next day or week's filming, putting together call sheets so the crew know when and where they are needed.

Script Supervisor – aka Continuity, tracks everything that happens during filming, making sure actors speak all their lines, that there are no continuity errors; also times and keeps a log of shots for the Editor to use later.

Camera Operator – the person working the camera, keeping the action in frame and following it as it progresses, working closely with the Director and the Director of Photography to capture their vision on film.

Focus Puller – assists the Camera Operator, making sure the shot stays in focus, changing lenses, adjusting the focus during the shot; is also responsible for the maintenance of the cameras.

Gaffer – the chief electrician on the set, responsible for lighting, working under the Director of Photography and managing other electricians on the set.

Continuity cock-ups

- *The Wizard of Oz.* 'During the sequence where Dorothy meets the Scarecrow, Dorothy's pigtails were first short (above her shoulders) and as the song progresses her hair gets longer (below her shoulders), then short, and then long again.'
- *Star Wars.* 'The first interior shot of the Millennium Falcon's cockpit shows small hanging dice. In every other shot, however, the dice are gone.'
- *Titanic.* 'Why, oh why is one of the people getting on the life boats wearing a digital watch? Surely they weren't around in 1912?'

(*Source: Movie Mistakes at www.moviemistakes.com*)

Best Boy or Girl – an electrician, second in charge of lighting after the Gaffer, responsible for ordering and co-ordinating the lighting equipment, setting it up and maintaining it.

Grip – in charge of the equipment that moves and lifts cameras during a shot, so lays tracks for the camera, operates cranes and dollies; if a Key Grip, manages the other Grips.

Art Director – works under the Production Designer, responsible for the designing of sets and their construction, in charge of running the whole art department and its budget.

Set Decorator – aka Set Dresser, decorates and furnishes the set, 'dressing' it with props, making sure it is 'dressed' on time for the shoot.

Graphic Designer – designs opening titles and credits, but also graphics for props, signs and anything else on camera, including visual effects.

JARGON BUSTER

Dolly
A cart that the camera, and sometimes camera crew, sit on during a shot, allowing the camera to move smoothly from one place to another, following the action. Sometimes there is a Dolly Grip, specifically in charge of the dolly.

For more Grip-speak, check out the Griptionary on the MSE Studio Equipment homepage (www.matthewsgrip.com).

Construction Manager – heads the set construction team, working closely with the Production Designer to make sure everything is built how it was designed.

Carpenters, Painters and Plasterers – do any carpentry, decorating and plastering work required on the set, working under the Construction Manager and for the art department.

Property Master or Mistress – in charge of researching, finding and managing all the props used by the actors, everything from handbags to coffee cups, spectacles to remote controls.

Make-up and Hair Designer – make-up and hair chief, researching and designing make-up and hair, and managing the make-up team, sometimes experts in specialist wigs and prosthetic special effects.

> **MY EXPERIENCE – MAKE-UP AND HAIR DESIGNER**
>
> 'Some people specialise in hair or make-up. I prefer to do both so I can shape the whole character ... I've been in the business 20 years and I'm still experimenting. On a documentary I did about the plague I had to make up boils which would ooze puss. I had no idea how to make puss so I spent some of the pre-production period working out how to do it. I once made a prosthetic nose for Judi Dench ... Research is essential, even for modern stuff. Apart from finding out technical information on a given period, research provides inspiration.'
>
> *Veronica Brebner, Make-up and Hair Designer*
> *(Source: Channel 4's Making Movies at*
> *www.channel4.com/film/makingmovies)*
>
>

Make-up and Hair Artist – does the actors' make-up before and during filming; nowadays often expected to style and trim hair as well.

Sound Recordist – aka the Production Sound Mixer, records the sound during filming, listening though headphones and working closely with the Boom Operator.

Boom Operator – holds the microphone boom, a long pole with a microphone attached, during filming, following the actors' movements, making sure the microphone is kept out of shot.

Dubbing Mixer – aka Re-Recording Mixer, merges and tinkers with all the sound elements on the film's sound track – the dialogue, background sound, sound effects and music - perfecting the final soundtrack.

Visual Effects Supervisor – aka Visual Effects Designer, creates visual effects and runs the visual effects team, designing effects either created live in front of the camera or superimposed later in post-production.

Unit Publicity – organises publicity while the film is being shot, setting up interviews with the cast and arranging for journalists to visit the set.

For more on what different people do in different departments, see Still Not Sure? (Chapter 5).

THE RIGHT PERSON FOR THE JOB

If you could have worked on *Bend it Like Beckham*, which job would you have done? Before you get carried away with fantasies about yourself as the Director, shouting 'and cut' at a large crew, or start daydreaming about yourself as a hot-shot Producer making your Oscar acceptance speech, have a think about which of these descriptions sounds most like you.

WHICH ONE ARE YOU?
1. **You are Mr or Mrs Calm**. You can do five things at the same time. You have strength and stamina, but you're also agile. Even after a long, tiring day, your powers of concentration are amazing – you're not easily distracted and you have a sharp eye for detail. You don't mind being given orders, even when you know they're not the right ones. You like being with a small team of people. Oh, and you're also a bit of a techie at heart – you spend hours messing around with new bits of equipment, working out how they work.
2. **You're an ideas person**. You're always on the look-out for new ones, in books, papers and magazines. Once you've hit on a great idea you really believe in, you stick with it. You take risks and you're supremely confident. You have the gift of the gab. You're a natural at selling and you don't mind asking people massive favours. You can juggle a hundred things at the same time and are as cool as a cucumber in a crisis. But, as well as being confident, you don't mind taking a backseat, letting others take the glory. You've got a gift for spotting talent.
3. **You're a rock**. You are the most reliable person you know – if you say you're going to be somewhere, you're there, on time. If you say you're going to do something, you do it. You're unbelievably organised, brilliant at planning and thinking ahead. You can spot potential problems a mile off. You also have strong nerves and don't particularly mind when people don't like you. You have the authority (and a loud enough voice) to get people to do what you tell them to. That said, you're also sensitive enough to be able to read the mood of a room.
4. **You have a great eye**. Everywhere you go, you notice how things look. You have a good visual memory – you remember small things you saw

ages ago. You have a strong sense of when things do and don't look right. You're also interested in how things are made and where they come from. You like research. You're good with your hands, at making something out of nothing – if you're stuck for a friend's birthday present, you have no problem cobbling together something imaginative at the last minute. You're creative and resourceful. And, on top of all that, you're organised and diplomatic.

5. **You love going to the cinema**. You always watch the Oscars on telly and read about Cannes in the papers – you love the stars, the dresses, the sheer glamour of the movies. You read *Heat* every week, without fail. You're good with people, a confident talker with positive body language. You're a born traveller. You love your life and work to be highly sociable. You like helping ambitious people get where they want to go, but you'd like to be famous yourself one day too.

6. **You're a born problem-solver**. You're great at creating calm order out of a chaotic mess. You like fiddling around with things for hours on end, often on your own. You don't much care where you work, because you're too busy concentrating. You can store a lot of information in your head. You are methodical, but you're also creative – you have a natural sense of pace, of rhythm, of how things should flow. You're also very diplomatic – when someone's upset, you're good at gently suggesting a solution, but don't mind if your idea gets vetoed.

THE JOBS THAT WOULD SUIT YOU

1. Looks like you might make a good **Camera Operator** or, at first, a **Focus Puller** and **Clapper Loader**. Camera Operators are highly skilled and some projects require a lot of creativity, but they don't always get much credit for what they do – the Director takes that, even when he or she doesn't deserve it. That's where the diplomacy comes in. Camera Operators often have to take orders from Directors who don't know what they're talking about – they give them the wrong instructions and then don't notice that the rushes only came out all right because the Camera Operator saved their bacon. At the same time as being led by a Director, the Camera Operator also needs to be a leader, looking after the camera team and making sure they're getting their jobs right.

2. How about being a **Producer**? And if not a Producer, a **Line Producer**, a **Production Manager** or a **Production Co-ordinator**? People who are good at these jobs are, essentially, great managers – of money, resources and, most of all, people. Producers are also highly creative. They scout around for ideas and talent, often coming up with the

concept for the film. But they are also good at business – they know how to raise money and sell ideas. All in all, it's a job for entrepreneurs. If you've got that entrepreneurial spirit – if you are always thinking up projects and clever ways to get them off the ground – this could be for you.

3. You'd make an ideal **First Assistant Director**: 1st ADs are the Director's rock – they are his or her eyes, ears and voice on the set, shouting out orders to the crew and keeping discipline on the set. They are also intimately involved in planning the filming – it's the 1st AD who puts together the schedule and he or she has to take the rap if it doesn't work out, if there's a big problem they should have seen coming. If things go wrong, it's up to them to fix it. While they need to be firm with people, pushing them to do their jobs properly and on time, they also need to be sensitive enough to know what the mood of the crew is, and when they're pushing people too far.

4. Come out of the closet – you'd be ideal working in wardrobe. In other words, you'd make a fine **Costume Designer**, **Supervisor**, **Maker** or **Assistant**. Obviously, you'll need to love clothes. (If not, how about working with props? It requires similar talents.) Costume staff need to come up with ideas and then make them happen. That means doing research, or trawling your visual memory bank for ideas, and then making them a reality, either by making the costumes or finding them somewhere else. They also need to be diplomats – they work closely with actors – and be very organised: putting together the costumes for a large cast is a massive job.

5. If only there were a job to fit this bill. You might, eventually, find a job that takes you to exotic places, to meet exotic people, but chances are you'll also have to work very, very hard in that job. Film crews do go to the Bahamas, but with the hours they work, they don't get much time on the beach or at the bar. You might also meet famous people, but working with them is different from hanging out with them. And yes, there can be great camaraderie, but it can also be highly stressful and when you're starting out people often treat you like a nobody. None of this means film isn't for you – just go into it with your eyes open, aware that it's hard work, in a tough industry.

6. Maybe you should think about editing. **Editors** need to love everything technical, messing around with new equipment and software. But they also need a strong creative streak. They're not just technicians – senior ones are considered as important as the Director when it comes to shaping the film and its feel. Editors need to be able to help the Director

get the film he or she wants from the rushes, fixing thousands of problems along the way, sometimes holding their hand while they do it. It may sound like a minor point – but it's worth stressing that Editors work long hours in dark, windowless rooms, so this is not a job for outdoors types.

HOW THEY GOT THERE

So how do you become a Producer or a Director of Photography? How did Costume Designers or Editors get where they are today? Here are some career route maps to give you a general idea of how some film industry professionals climb the greasy pole. Remember, though, people take all kinds of different routes, often switching direction as they go.

Director
Writer, Editor, Director of Photography, Producer, Actor, Assistant Director → Director

Producer
Writer, Director, Funder → Producer

Producer
Office Runner→Production Secretary or Receptionist→Production Assistant→Production Co-ordinator→Production Manager→Producer

Director of Photography
Runner or Trainee→Clapper Loader/Camera Assistant→Focus Puller→Camera Operator→Lighting Cameraman→Director of Photography

Editor
Post-Production Runner→Assistant Editor→Editor→Supervisory Editor

Production Designer
Art and Design student→Runner→Art Department Assistant→ Assistant Art Director→Art Director→Production Designer

Costume Designer
Fashion/Costume/Theatre student→Wardrobe Assistant→Costume Design Assistant→Wardrobe Mistress/Master→Costume Supervisor→Costume Designer

Construction Manager
Training (carpentry, plastering, decorating)→Trainee Crafts Person→ Craft Person→Craft Supervisor→Assistant Construction Manager→ Construction Manager

Make-Up/Hair Designer
Beauty and Hair student→ Make-Up/Hair Assistant→Make-Up/Hair Artist→Make-Up/Hair Designer or Chief

Lighting Director
Trained electrician→Lighting Assistant→Electrician or Lighting Operator→Best Boy→Gaffer→Lighting Director

Sound Supervisor
Runner or Trainee→Sound Assistant→Boom Operator→Sound Recordist or Mixer→Sound Supervisor

'Do you want to work in a creative or technical job? Do you want to work behind the scenes or in front of them? Do you want to be someone who helps make films happen?'

what you need to be, how to get there

If you know you want to work in film, but still don't know which job is for you, maybe you need to think more generally about which *area* of the film industry you would like to be in, or what kind of department you would like to work in.

Do you want to work in a creative or technical job? Do you want to work behind the scenes or in front of them? Do you want to be someone who helps make films happen? Or someone who sells happening films to the public?

If you're still not sure, take a look at the four different areas you could go into:

1. Creative and Productive
2. Artistic
3. Technical
4. Business.

1. CREATIVE AND PRODUCTIVE

If you're creative, but not necessarily artistic, or if you're a natural born organiser, happy helping creative people do their thing, writing, producing or a job in production may be for you. Read on ...

WRITING
The jobs
Scriptwriter/Screenwriter, Script Developer, Script Editor, Script Reader.

What you need to be
Creative, imaginative. Patient, self-disciplined. A big reader. Able to take criticism.

What you need to have
Strong written and communication skills. A natural grasp of the English language. Good research skills, with an ability to think structurally.

 MY EXPERIENCE – SCRIPT EDITOR

'I work on film projects through their development stage – often from the inception of an idea, through the scripting process with the writer (and director) and into production. Though the core of the work is developing the script, the job also entails talent scouting – attending short films, the theatre, etc – and the constant search for new ideas. On an average day I will read one or two scripts. The working environment is comfortable, relaxed and so creative. What can be frustrating is the often slow nature of development work – it's exciting when a project you're working on goes ahead into production, but you're not guaranteed to be working on something that is going to be made.'

Sam, Script Editor

How to get there

There is only one way to become a writer – start writing: short stories, treatments, scripts for short films, and then feature-length ones. Most Scriptwriters work in both film and TV, although they are often also novelists, playwrights or journalists.

Some wannabe Scriptwriters start out as Script Readers, writing reports on scripts for Producers, going on to become Script Editors. Others become Script Readers and Editors because they want to become Producers. If you want to be a Scriptwriter, it's largely self-taught, but there are a growing number of good courses in scriptwriting.

PRODUCING AND PRODUCTION
The jobs

Executive Producer, Producer, Director, Line Producer, Associate Producer, Assistant Producer, Production Manager, Location Manager, Location Assistant/Assistant Location Manager, Casting Director, Casting Assistant/Associate, Script Supervisor/Continuity, Production Co-ordinator, Production Assistant, First/Second/Third Assistant Director, Production Secretary/Supervisor, Runner.

What you need to be

Organised, methodical. A good talker and listener, with strong interpersonal skills. Tactful and able to work under pressure. For more senior roles, a born leader.

What you need to have

Research, organisational and administrative skills.

How to get there

Most newcomers start out as runners and work their way up, becoming Production Assistants and/or Assistant Directors, and then maybe Production Co-ordinators and Production Managers, and eventually Producers. Some go into other areas of Production – Location Management or Casting. Almost everyone learns on the job, although some do film-related NVQs, degrees and MAs. There are short courses in Production and Skillset qualifications that can be done while working.

" MY EXPERIENCE

'I got my first job as a fill-in – one day covering for another runner at a pop promos company. I then became their regular fill-in, running around Soho doing errands, and then – eventually – their runner. It can all seem like a long haul, but there are people who start running in their early 20s and are Producers by their late 20s.'

Karen, Runner

'To become a Production Co-ordinator, the usual route is to start as a Runner then work as Secretary on a few jobs. I got into the industry in my late 20's as a Production assistant then did two jobs as Secretary then moved on to Co-ordinating. There is no real training for production work – you do need to be highly organised, be able to multi-task, solve problems (of which there are many) and have good people skills.'

Sue, Production Co-ordinator

'I got my first job through friends. I got introduced to someone, did an interview and was then taken on, on trial, on very low pay. But, while I was working there, I made good friends with the Production Co-ordinator who has since got me a lot of work. By working on music videos and commercials you meet people who then get you work on features, when they come up.'

Laura, Production Assistant

"

2. ARTISTIC

If you're lucky enough to have the creative gene, how about working in one of these? Art and Design, Costume/Wardrobe, Make-up and Hair, Set Crafts, Special Effects and Animation.

ART AND DESIGN
The jobs
Production Designer, Art Director/Design Assistant/Assistant Designer, Set Designer, Assistant Art Director, Graphic Designer, Model Maker, Props Master/Mistress, Props/Production Buyer, Scenic Artist, Set Decorator/Dresser, Art Department Runner.

What you need to be
Creative, artistic, imaginative. Patient, resourceful, precise. A good talker (and listener). Well organised. Happy to present your work to other people. A collaborator, good at working in a team.

What you need to have
Good drawing and design skills and, in some roles, computer skills.

How to get there
Most people enter the job market with an Art and Design degree, often in a related field such as Theatre Design or Interior Design. Some have a degree in architecture. A common first job is Art Department Runner, with people working their way up to Art Director, aka Assistant Designer or Design Assistant and then, maybe, Production Designer.

COSTUME AND WARDROBE
The jobs
Costume Designer, Wardrobe Master/Mistress or Costume/Wardrobe Supervisor, Costume Design Assistant/Assistant Costume Designer, Costumier, Costume Maker, Wardrobe Assistant, Dresser.

What you need to be
Interested in costume, art, design, film and literature. Organised, enthusiastic, tactful, diplomatic, adaptable. A calm and communicative team worker.

What you need to have
Hand and sewing machine skills, a good knowledge of fabrics and sewing techniques, sound research skills.

How to get there
A foundation course in Art and Design, followed by a degree in fashion, costume or theatre design is the norm. Lots of people start out in theatre and then move into film. Many get their first job as a Wardrobe Assistant, working their way up to become Costume Design Assistant, Costume Supervisor and then Costume Designer. Some start out working for costume hire companies as Costumiers or Costume Buyers.

MAKE-UP AND HAIR
The jobs
Make-up Designer/Artist or Make-up Chief/Supervisor, Make-up Artist/Make-up and Hair, Make-up Effects/Special Effect Make-up Artist/Prosthetics, Hairdresser, Hairdressing Assistant, Make-up/Hair Assistant or Trainee, Wig Specialist.

What you need to be
Creative and artistic. Patient, resourceful and good on details. A confident communicator, skilled at putting people at ease. Happy to work under pressure.

What you need to have
Good working knowledge of make-up and hair styles, techniques and products, as well as about the effects of lighting and cameras on the skin and hair. Research skills and specialist make-up knowledge.

How to get there
A hairdressing, make-up and beauty degree, plus on-the-job training and experience. Some training schemes require NVQ level 2 in Beauty Therapy and NVQ level 2 in Hair Dressing. After training, a first job might be as a junior Make-up Assistant, moving on to Make-up Assistant and eventually Make-up Designer/Artist. Some people specialise in either Make-up or Hair, others do both – with a general tightening of budgets, there is a definite trend towards multi-skilling.

Visual FX

Visual Effects workers in the UK are some of the most highly rated in the world, which is why more and more international filmmakers are coming here to get effects done – *Saving Private Ryan*, *Gladiator*, the Harry Potter and Bond movies are just some of the recent films with UK-made effects.

'The British visual effects community has some of the most talented people in the industry,' says Ridley Scott, an English director who has used plenty of effects in his films – *Gladiator*, *Alien* and *Blade Runner*.

It's a small (about 650 people) but thriving industry. Here are some of the very specialist areas Special or Visual Effects professionals work in:

- Pyrotechnics – from large-scale explosions to small fireworks, anything that explodes live in front of the camera.
- Physical Effects – snow, rain, a tornado, an erupting volcano or any other natural disaster a film might need.
- Sculpture and Animatronics – think monsters and mummies, dinosaurs and anything else scary-looking.
- Miniatures – animals, people, landscapes, spacecraft, or anything else that is too big or difficult to build but that could be created by using miniatures and scale models.
- Special Props – anything from robots to those sugar glass bottles so often smashed over actors' heads.
- 3D Animation and Digital Effects – creating worlds that don't exist, or that are too hard and expensive to get to ie, outer space.

For detailed information on the Visual Effects industry and how to get in, see the skillsformedia website at www.skillsformedia.com.

SET CRAFTS
The jobs
Construction Manager, Carpenter, Joiner, Set Painter and Decorator, Plasterer, Wood Working Assistant

What you need to be
A good team worker, with sound communication and interpersonal skills. Happy to give and receive orders.

What you need to have
Practical and technical skills, good knowledge of health and safety, physical strength.

How to get there
Most people are already qualified in their trade when they come into the profession, although some learn and train on the job, for example by doing Skillset/Construction Industry Training Board (CITB) NVQs.

ANIMATION
The Jobs
Animation Director, Key Animator, Animator, 3D Animator, Animation Producer, Layout Artist, Compositor, Storyboard Artist, Model Maker, Character Designer, Cartoonist, Special Effects Animator, Background Painter, Animation Assistant/Assistant Animator, Animation Production Runner, In-betweener.

What you need to be
Creative, imaginative, patient, precise. Resourceful, enthusiastic, organised. A problem-solver, as well as a good communicator and team worker.

What you need to have
Sound drawing skills, good (often specialist) computer know-how. Good art and design knowledge.

How to get there
About 57 per cent of people going into animation have an animation-related degree, and another 25 per cent have an equivalent animation-related

Some of the major players in UK animation and digital visual effects are:

- Aardman (http://aardman.com) – *Wallace & Gromit*, *Chicken Run*, *Angry Kid* and *Rex the Runt*
- Cosgrove Hall (www.chf.co.uk) – *Dangermouse*, *Count Duckula*, *Bill and Ben*
- Moving Picture Company (www.moving-picture.com) – *Harry Potter*, *Tomb Raider* and *Helen of Troy*
- FramestoreCFC (www.framestorecfc.co.uk) – visual effects on *Harry Potter & the Chamber of Secrets*, *Walking with Dinosaurs*
- Mill Films (www.mill.co.uk) – visual effects on *Gladiator*, *Tomb Raider*, *A Knight's Tale*.

qualification, according to a Skillset Animation Industry survey carried out in 1997/8. Some go on to do postgraduate courses too, although on-the-job experience is more important.

3. TECHNICAL

If you have techie tendencies, you might want to think about doing something with cameras, lights, sound or some of the other technical jobs in film. Some Camera workers and Editors might be a bit miffed to be in the 'technical' section – what many of them do, especially those in more senior jobs, is both highly technical and highly creative. That said, everyone in Camera and Editing works their way up from the bottom, and the jobs are much more technical than creative at first.

CAMERA
The jobs
Director of Photography/Cinematographer, Lighting Cameraman, Camera Supervisor/Senior Cameraman, Camera Operator, Focus Puller/First Assistant Cameraman, Clapper Loader/Second Assistant Cameraman/Camera Assistant, Grip.

What you need to be
Creative and precise. A good communicator. Well disciplined and, at more senior levels, a leader.

What you need to have
Experience and interest in still photography. Good working knowledge of cameras. Strong awareness of health and safety. Physical fitness.

How to get there
Many people working in Camera Departments start out as Clapper Loaders, going on to become Focus Pullers and then Camera Operators and maybe Lighting Cameramen. There are also training opportunities for new entrants at the BBC or FT2, as well as courses that can be done on the job. A degree in photography, graphic design or media may help.

LIGHTING
The jobs
Lighting Director, Gaffer, Best Boy, Electrician/Lighting Operator, Lighting Assistant.

What you need to be
Patient, precise, careful. A good communicator and team worker.

What you need to have
Working knowledge of lighting equipment. Physical fitness and stamina, a good head for heights.

How to get there
Most lighting experts enter the profession as qualified electricians, and learn the rest on the job.

SOUND
The jobs
Sound Recordist/Production Mixer, Boom Operator, Sound Assistant, Sound Technician, Dubbing Mixer, Sound Editor, Dialogue Editor, Music Editor, Foley Editor, Foley Artist.

What you need to be
Passionate about sound, technically minded, a good communicator. Patient and precise.

What you need to have
Good hearing, good balance, good fitness levels. Knowledge about sound equipment and recording techniques. Experience in radio or music.

How to get there
Relevant qualifications are not a must, although a degree in physics, electronics, electrical engineering or music can help. There are specialist short courses for beginners. Most people learn – and train – on the job. A common first job is as a Runner and then Sound Assistant, helping out the Sound Recordist and Boom Operator.

CLASSIC SOUND CLICHÉS

- Thunder is always in sync with lightning.
- Whenever someone speaks into a microphone, their first words will cause the mic to feed back.
- People standing next to a running helicopter can always talk in normal, or just slightly louder than normal, voices.
- Guns have a really deep 'BOOOOMMM!!' sound, not a 'CRACK!'

(*Source: Film Sound* (www.filmsound.org), *a site all about sound in film.*

MY EXPERIENCE

'I started out in student and then independent radio, and then got a chance to do some training through some Scottish Screen funding. I was attached to a feature film production in Shepperton as an apprentice. My training was all in film, but I after I finished, the bottom dropped out of the film industry, so I went straight into non-broadcast video production, doing corporate stuff – which I still think is a great way in. There aren't many people who only do films. It would be very hard to survive financially – you'd need to be getting work on three or four features a year, which would be difficult.'

Becky, Sound Recordist and Boom Operator

POST-PRODUCTION
The jobs
Post-Production Supervisor/Co-ordinator, Picture Editor, Film Editor/Offline Editor, Videotape Editor, Assistant Film Editor (First/Second/Third), Colour Grader, Runner.

What you need to be
Calm, patient, precise. Well organised. Good at working with people, often in dark, small spaces.

What you need to have
Computer skills. Knowledge of digital editing techniques. A good visual sense, an eye for detail and a feel for music and rhythm.

How to get there
Some start out as Runners for Post-Production companies, working their way up to become an Assistant Editor and then Editor. Editors on major feature films usually have years of experience, and are regarded as playing one of the most creative roles in the production process. Most of those

making their way up the ladder work on TV projects and commercials most of the time. There aren't many relevant degree courses, or at least ones where editing is the primary focus, but there are some entry-level training schemes, as well as training opportunities for people once they have entered the profession.

4. BUSINESS

Don't assume a career in film only means directing, producing or camerawork – there are loads of 'hidden' jobs in film, in finance, distribution, publicity, sales and marketing and finance.

FINANCE
The most common finance job in film is as a Production Accountant, the person who manages a film's budget. Production Accountants need to be good with numbers, well organised and able to work under pressure. A first step is to become an Assistant Production Accountant. Training is available, most prestigiously on the Assistant Production Accountant Training Scheme run by the Production Guild.

DISTRIBUTION, SALES, PUBLICITY AND MARKETING
There are only about 250 people working for UK film distribution companies, according to the Film Distributors' Association (FDA). But many more work in distribution indirectly, for advertising, PR and design agencies that have distributors as clients.

Film PR

The publicity for films is either done in-house by distributors or handed out to public relations agencies. Here's what they do:

- Unit Publicity – co-ordinating publicity while the film is being made, getting photos taken and taking journalists to the set, to do interviews and get some early publicity for the project.
- Release Publicity – in the run-up to the film's release, organising screenings, setting up interviews with actors and directors, getting features placed in the press.
- Corporate Publicity – publicity for film companies, getting press coverage for them and their projects.

The distribution business

'Usually, feature films open first theatrically (in cinemas), where they can have the greatest impact, looking and sounding their best. After the theatrical window, films are next released on home video/DVD, then on various forms of pay television and finally, two or three years after opening in cinemas, on free-to-air television, where they may enjoy many repeat screenings.

'There are a number of "major" UK film distribution companies (affiliated to the big Hollywood studios) and "independent" (unaffiliated) distributors, who tend to handle films made outside the studios or niche titles. Any film distribution company may compete for the right to release locally produced films.

'The role of distribution, which often begins even before shooting gets underway, is to draw the widest possible audience to each individual film, realising the full potential of the filmmakers' work. Each new release has its own sales and marketing strategy, tailored and developed in conjunction with the producers and/or parent studio. There are very few hard and fast rules. Distributors must sell the films they are launching to: exhibitors, the media, marketing partners and the public.'

(*From the Film Distributors' Association. See its website, Launching Films* (www.launchingfilms.co.uk), *for more info on film distribution, from the latest film releases to advice on working in distribution.*)

The jobs
Acquisitions, Sales (Sales Manager, Sales Representative), Marketing (Marketing Manager), Publicity (Press Officer, Publicity Assistant).

What you need to be
Passionate about film. A natural salesperson – able to persuade and inspire people to buy or promote a product. A team worker.

What you need to have
Experience in sales, marketing or PR.

How to get there

To get into film marketing, the FDA recommends getting experience in an advertising or media planning agency firm, ideally one with film or entertainment clients. For careers in film publicity, experience as a journalist or press officer, in another field, will help. Most film publicists work for PR agencies, not distributors. Sales staff, who deal with the licensing of individual films to the cinemas, may also come in from sales jobs in other fields. That said, there are people who come straight into distribution, getting jobs as office assistants and then learning the trade on the job.

'The trick is to get as much training and work experience as you can. You're also going to have to make some friends. Film people work in a close-knit community – friends hire friends and personal recommendations are everything.'

6. GETTING IN

networking, training, doing it for yourself

So now you know what jobs are out there, how are you going to get one? Breaking into the film industry is tough and even when you're in, it goes on being tough. Working in film nearly always means working freelance, so it's not just a question of getting your first job, but the one after that, and the one after that.

Even once you're on your way, getting regular work, you'll need to keep networking and, just as importantly, training – especially as lots of the best training opportunities in film are only open to people *already* working in the business.

Another crucial bit of advice: be flexible. Not many people working in film work exclusively in film. There just aren't enough films being made. Most people flit continually between features and shorts, TV shows, commercials, pop promos and corporate jobs. If you want to make a living, you're going to have to be open-minded.

" INSIDERS' TIPS ON GETTING IN

'I didn't go to film school. It's not a must. But, if you can get into one and afford it, it gives you a chance to try things out, to make mistakes and to find like-minded people to grow with.'

Pawel Pawlikowski, documentary maker
and feature writer-director, including Last Resort

'Apply relentlessly to all the vacancies you can find. Put whatever experience you can on your CV – anything that demonstrates your enthusiasm. Don't be put off. You will get knocked back a lot, but don't worry about it. Many websites let you post your details for free and producers and production managers will often come looking for you that way. I personally do not believe in doing large CV mail-outs, or going round production companies and hand-delivering them. I'm sure it has worked for some people, but in my experience it doesn't.'

Josh, Runner

'There is no set way in. It does still depend, to some extent, on knowing someone involved in the film industry. If you want to be a Clapper Loader, you need to find a focus puller or clapper loader who wants to have a trainee around, which basically means going along on shoots and helping out the camera department. This is generally unpaid but is a great way to learn all the kit. Working on student films is also a way of meeting camera crews. There are always far more people wanting to do it than there are jobs and I think in the end you have to be really lucky. When you do get work as a trainee you have to be as keen as possible and make lots of tea!'

Kate, Clapper Loader

'Courses are good for getting motivated. It can be very hard to get going on your own. Personally, I didn't do any – I felt that if I saw how many people were out there, writing scripts, I'd feel like I didn't stand a chance. Start by writing an episode for a soap or a short film.

There are loads of short film schemes you can apply for. Or try and get someone at film school to make it. It doesn't matter if what you write at first doesn't get made – it's your calling card to get you other work. Once you've got a script you want to show people, write to people you admire in the business and ask if they'll look at it. Or go to events they're speaking at. Everyone is always looking for talent.'

Amy Jenkins, Screenwriter, including
This Life *and* Elephant Juice

'Get a good art training – in drawing, painting, history of art, sculpture. Find an inspiring designer to work for and offer your services to them. Find out where they're working and try to meet them face-to-face. When you get a job, always ask if you don't understand something. Take notes in meetings. Ideas have to be tangible. You also have to be flexible – filming changes all the time due to many factors. It's not for the faint-hearted. Always have an A–Z, a personal reference library of pictures that interest you and a copy of the *Knowledge* – a directory of everybody and everything you will need.'

Alison Dominitz, Production Designer

'Get a job as an Office Runner and then, if you can, as a Production Assistant. You need to try and get a Producer or Production Manager to take you under their wing. If you do well in your first PA job, if they know they can trust you, they'll often take you with them to their next job. A lot of people also start in reception jobs at production companies. It's a good way of meeting people, although it can be hard to move on.'

Laura, Production Assistant

'If people are really interested in getting into this industry then the best thing they can do is start doing it at home. If you've got access to a computer and can play around with some cheap animation software – there's free software you can get your hands on (try www.tucows.net) – play around and see what you can do. What people should be doing is working towards producing a showreel, which is just getting some work onto a tape. It could be 30 seconds' worth of work ... It should be concise and really show your talent!'

Matt Aitken, 3D Animator
*(Source: **IDEAS**FACTORY at www.channel4.com/ideasfactory)*

TRAINING, QUALIFICATIONS AND COURSES

There are hundreds of film-related qualifications and courses out there. Sadly, there aren't nearly as many jobs, so if you are going to train – especially if you're paying for it yourself – it's important you do the right kind of training on the right kind of course.

Finding out about training opportunities and courses is in itself a full-time job. There are so many professional bodies, industry organisations and course providers, it can all feel a bit overwhelming. Let's kick off with some of the basic, frequently asked questions.

FAQs
What should I study?
It depends what you want to do in film and whether you're planning to go to university. If you are, you'll need to get enough relevant A-levels to do the course you want, so think about what kind of degree you're interested in, and which A-levels are recommended for those courses. Media or Film Studies is not a must, at GCSE or A-level, but try and find out if the university courses you're interested in prefer you to have them. As a general rule, you should do what you're most interested in, what you love – it doesn't matter if it's not directly related to film.

For some jobs, especially in art, design and construction, you might be in a stronger position later if you take General National Vocational Qualifications (GNVQs) and Advanced GNVQs, aka Vocational A-levels, rather than traditional A-levels. These give you more practical experience. However, if you are planning to go on to university, make sure the courses you're interested in rate Advanced GNVQs as highly as A-levels.

If you're thinking of doing something technical in film, it's probably a good idea to get some maths and/or physics qualifications. Even if you're not planning to do any further education, GCSEs in these subjects may give you a head start when you're applying for training or jobs.

Do I need a degree?

You definitely don't *have* to have a degree to work in film. Instead, you could get NVQs or SVQs, a Modern Apprenticeship or a Foundation degree, relevant to whatever it is you want to do. There are also some very good new entrant training schemes open to over-18s. But be warned – you'll have to fight to get a place and many applicants are over-qualified.

Although you don't need a degree to get on a training scheme, or to get a job, lots of people applying have them. Fifty-five per cent of people working freelance in feature films have a degree, and 32 per cent also have a postgraduate qualification, according to the Skillset Freelance Survey.

Even so, having a degree won't necessarily put you at an advantage. There is a growing feeling, now that so many people coming into film have degrees, and often media-related ones, that they are not worth as much as they used to be. FT2, the most highly rated new entrant training scheme in the business, says because 90 per cent of applicants have studied some form of media-related programme, they are 'more interested in what applicants have done, over and above studying, to find their own way into the industry'.

There are some jobs you *will* need a degree for. For example, for many art and design jobs, an art degree is a basic requirement. Likewise for some

Vital stats

More than 25,000 people are studying over 700 media-related courses at first degree and postgraduate level, at more than 400 different institutions across the UK. There are also more than 5,000 students studying media-related courses in sixth forms in England and Wales. The good news is that 76 per cent of media graduates find work within six months of graduation, compared to 69 per cent of all graduates.

(Sources: *Skills for Tomorrow's Media: The Report of the Skillset/DCMS Audio Visual Industries Training Group, September 2001; Association of Graduate Careers Advisory Service*)

Getting advice

- **IDEAS**FACTORY has an online advice service, in association with learndirect, answering questions about training and careers in the creative industries. See the Training and Courses section at www.channel4.com/ideasfactory.
- Anyone aged up to 19 in England can get advice on qualifications and courses from **Connexions**, the support service for young people. See the Connexions website (www.connexions.gov.uk) for information and to find out where your local Connexions Service is.
- **skillsformedia** is a brilliant source of advice for new entrants, students and people already working in film. Its website has loads of information on careers, qualifications and training. See www.skillsformedia.com.

highly specialist, technical jobs, a science degree is the norm. This is something you will need to really research. See Getting Advice, above.

Bear in mind that, apart from qualifications, there are other important things a degree can give you. Further education develops your mind, teaching you to think more critically and analytically. Maybe even more important, it gives you time – time to think about what you want to do in life, time to have a laugh making student films, get some work experience in the holidays, and to develop your social skills. Finding a job and working in film is all about confidence, getting on with people and being able to cope with the ups and downs of freelance life – life skills not everyone has when they're fresh out of school.

Should I do a media degree?
Not necessarily. Nearly 25 per cent of freelancers working on feature films have a media-related degree, according to the Skillset Freelance Survey. Slightly more – 32 per cent – have a non-media-related degree. 'A degree in media studies is not essential,' says PACT, the Producers Alliance for Cinema and Television. 'The best media studies degrees with a vocational bias are generally at postgraduate level ... Another degree such as law,

business or a language might offer you more flexibility.' In other words, you might be better off doing a non-vocational first degree, followed by a vocational postgraduate degree.

If you are thinking about a media-related degree, it needs to be one with a strong practical, vocational element to it. It's important to understand the difference between Media Studies degrees and Media degrees. Media Studies degrees tend to be purely academic and theoretical, analysing the role of the media in society, whereas Media or Media Production degrees are more practical, teaching professional skills. See Choosing the Right Course on page 79.

Can't I just learn on the job?

Yes. You could get a job as a Runner (see page 35) or trainee, for example, and work your way up. Film has a strong tradition of people starting at the very bottom and slowly working their way up. Having a degree doesn't necessarily help you climb the ladder any faster – everyone starts out at the bottom of the heap.

That said, you will need to do training while you're working. Until recently, because so much of film is freelance, on-the-job training has been a bit haphazard – people picked up whatever skills they could, doing the odd course here and there. Now vocational qualifications, and in particular the Skillset Professional Qualifications, which are NVQs and SVQs you get while working, are taken seriously. In future, they may be a must for anyone wanting to move up the career ladder. See Vocational Qualifications on page 77.

What they studied

When Skillset did a survey of freelances working in the audio-visual industries, it asked them whether they had studied and if so, what. Here's what freelances working on feature films, commercials, corporate production and animation said:

	Features (%)	Commercials (%)
Media-related degree	23	30
Other degree	32	33
Media-related postgraduate degree	21	13
Other postgraduate degree	11	7
Relevant technical qualification	24	22
Other technical qualification	14	7
NVQ	6	8
Modern Apprenticeship	3	1

	Corporate (%)	Animation (%)
Media-related degree	28	41
Other degree	33	24
Media-related postgraduate degree	14	30
Other postgraduate degree	14	12
Relevant technical qualification	26	12
Other technical qualification	11	6
NVQ	13	6
Modern Apprenticeship	1	0

(*Source: Skillset Freelance Survey, January 2002*)

NEW-ENTRANT TRAINING SCHEMES

If you can get on to one of these, you'll be well on your way. New entrant schemes are formal training schemes, usually in specialist areas of film – camera, sound, wardrobe, etc. Trainees do short, highly focused vocational courses, but spend most of their time working on real films, in real jobs.

The bad news is that, according to skillsformedia, there are fewer than 100 places on all the training schemes put together – and thousands apply. 'Applicants that have done their homework on the industry, are keen and enthusiastic, know their area of specialisation, and perhaps already have some work experience, will stand a far better chance,' it advises.

The main schemes are described here.

Channel 4 Training Schemes

Channel 4 is one of the leading broadcasters in supporting and developing new talent in the audio-visual industries. The Channel places strong emphasis on nurturing and developing talent and contributes to film and television training through various independent organisations. These schemes range from music promo production to animation, from acting classes to trainee drama director opportunities, plus regional support schemes and support for disabled and hearing impaired people in the industry. Details of most of these schemes can be found on **IDEAS**FACTORY (www.channel4.com/ideasfactory).

In addition, every two years Channel 4 sponsors four people from ethnic minority backgrounds (to encourage diversity in the industry) on the Film & Television Freelance Training's (FT2) New Entrant Scheme, see below. This is a competitive and highly regarded scheme, which aims to get people into junior grades (in camera, sound, editing, etc) within the freelance industry.

FT2

FT2 – Film and Television Freelance Training – is the leading provider of training for new entrants to the industry. It is for over-18s who want to work freelance in the construction, production and technical areas of film and TV. Trainees do placements, short courses and Skillset NVQs. FT2 runs three different schemes:

1. *New Entrant Technical Training Programme*
   A two-year apprenticeship scheme, with 10–15 places a year, for newcomers wanting to do the following jobs:
   - Art Department Assistant
   - Assistant Editor
   - Assistant Location Manager
   - Camera Assistant/Clapper Loader
   - Grips
   - Make-up/Hair Assistant
   - Production Assistant
   - Props Assistant
   - Sound Assistant
   - Wardrobe Assistant.

2. *Set Crafts Apprenticeship Training Scheme*
   A two-year apprenticeship, with four to six places a year, for new
   entrants wanting to work in set construction, in these areas:
   ● Carpentry and Joinery
   ● Fibrous Plastering
   ● Set Painting and Decorating.

3. *Independent Companies Researcher Training Scheme*
   This is for new entrants, aged 20 plus, wanting to work as researchers
   in factual programming, so is essentially a TV training scheme. It takes
   six to eight people for an 18-month period.

For more information on FT2 schemes and advice on how to apply, see the
FT2 website or send an A4 SAE to FT2, Fourth Floor, Warwick House, 9
Warwick Street, London W1B 5LY. Website: www.ft2.org.uk.

Watch this space
In 2003, FT2 ran a pilot training scheme in Feature Film
Development. FT2 is currently evaluating it, and will be
deciding whether to run future training schemes for script
development in early 2004. See the website for an update:
www.ft2.org.uk.

The BBC
The BBC used to be the main training provider in the UK. It still trains
about 350 new recruits a year, but training schemes now tend to be offered
when the need arises, rather than year in, year out. All schemes are
advertised in the press and on the BBC's Job pages online
(www.bbc.co.uk/jobs), so keep an eye out. These are some of the schemes
they have been running recently:

● *Vision Design*
  A one-year scheme for young designers, with training and on-the-job
  experience. Selection is done through an annual Design Competition
  followed by assessed work attachments. The number of trainees varies
  from year to year, but for the 2003 intake there were 13 new trainees in art
  direction, costume design, make-up and new media design, plus two sent
  to broadcast graphics and interactive design departments. For more
  information, see the Vision Design website at www.bbc.co.uk/designvision.

- *Operational Trainees*
  The BBC's Operational Trainees are placed with BBC Resources Ltd, a commercial subsidiary of the BBC providing production facilities and design services – studios, outside broadcast units, post-production and design services. It is a two-year scheme. Trainees work in:
  - *Studios* specialising in either cameras, sound or lighting, with a view to employment as a Camera Operator, Sound Assistant or Vision Operator.
  - *Outside broadcasts* specialising in 'Obs', with a view to becoming a Technical Operator.
  - *Post-production* specialising in viewing, transferring, transmitting and digitising video and audio material, with a view to working as an Editor.

For more information, see the BBC Trainees section on the BBC Jobs website (www.bbc.co.uk/jobs).

Cyfle

Cyfle is the leading vocational training company for the film, television and interactive media industries in Wales. It has a full-time training scheme, lasting a year, with 18 places. Trainees are placed in production and facility companies in Wales. They also do short courses and are assessed for Skillset NVQs.

Contact: Cyfle, Gronant, Penrallt Isaf, Caernarfon, Gwynedd LL55 1NS, Tel: 01286 671 000, Email: cyfle@cyfle.co.uk, Website: www.cyfle.co.uk.

Scottish Screen

Scottish Screen, which develops, encourages and promotes film, television and new media in Scotland, runs an 18-month New Entrants Training Scheme. Trainees specialise in technical, craft, design and production areas, doing short courses, the Skillset Professional Qualifications at level 2 and placements in television production, commercials and feature films. In 2002, it took eight trainees, one in each of the following areas:

- Camera
- Production Factual
- Production Drama
- Assistant Directing
- Make-up
- Post-production
- Art Department
- Locations.

Contact: Scottish Screen, 2nd Floor, 249 West George St, Glasgow G2 4QE, Tel: 0141 302 1700, Email: nets@scottishscreen.com, Website: www.scottishscreen.com.

Northern Ireland Film and Television Commission

The Northern Ireland Film and Television Commission, an agency for the development of the film industry and film culture in Northern Ireland, runs the FOCUS programme, which provides work placements on local productions for trainees who want to learn new skills and develop existing ones. Trainees work within their chosen craft area, usually in an assistant grade, and are paid a weekly allowance. While on the placement, they are assigned a mentor. Interviews take place twice a year, although at the time of going to press, the scheme was 'on hold until further notice'.

Contact: Northern Ireland Film and Television Commission, 3rd Floor, Alfred House, 21 Alfred St, Belfast BT2 8ED, Tel: 028 9023 2444, Email: info@niftc.co.uk, Website: www.niftc.co.uk.

Michael Samuelson Lighting

A highly rated scheme for new entrants wanting to become lighting professionals. It takes up to ten trainees a year and places them throughout the film industry for a year. Applicants need to have basic electrical qualifications. Recruitment is in May and trainees start in July.

Contact: Michael Samuelson Lighting, Pinewood Studios, Iver Heath, Buckinghamshire SL0 0NH, Tel: 020 8795 7020.

Animator in Residence (AIR) scheme

Channel 4 and the British Film Institute run this scheme, offering four trainees the chance to do three-month residencies at the National Museum of Photography, Film & Television (www.nmpft.org.uk). Applicants need to be recent graduates (within the last five years) with an original idea for a three-minute animated film. At the end, they submit a proposal to Channel 4.

Contact: The AIR Scheme Administrator, BFI/NT, South Bank, Waterloo, London SE1 8XT, Tel: 020 7815 1376, Website: www.a-i-r.info.

Assistant Production Accountant Training Scheme

The Production Guild runs this scheme for new entrants wanting to become Assistant Production Accountants. It takes six trainees for 12 months. They do short courses, leading to the Skillset NVQ in Production

Accounting Level 3, and also work on big productions. In 2002, trainees worked on films including *Die Another Day*, *28 Days Later* and *Dirty Pretty Things*. They are paid a tax-free allowance of £300 a week. The Guild says 'applicants must possess either academic or vocational qualifications in accounting or be able to demonstrate that they have acquired an equivalent level of competence through their work experience, for example, as a cashier, bookkeeper, or in a junior financial administration capacity.'

Contact: The Production Guild, Pinewood Studios, Pinewood Road, Iver Heath, Bucks SL0 0NH, Tel: 01753 651767, Email: info@productionguild.com, Website: www.productionguild.com.

Other training opportunities for new entrants
There are other new entrant training schemes around the country. These are the organisations you should contact to ask for more information:

- **Media Training North West**, Room G082, BBC, Oxford Rd, Manchester M60 1SJ, Tel: 0161 244 4637, Email: info@mtnw.co.uk, Website: www.mtnw.co.uk.
- **Northern Film & Media**, Central Square, Forth St, Newcastle upon Tyne NE1 3PJ, Tel: 0191 269 9200, Website: www.northernmedia.org.
- **Screen Yorkshire**, 40 Hanover Square, Leeds LS3 1BQ, Tel: 0113 294 4410, Website: www.ysc.co.uk.
- **Screen West Midlands**, 31–41 Bromley Street, Birmingham B9 4AN, Tel: 0121 766 1470, Email: info@screenwm.co.uk, Website: www.screenwm.co.uk.
- **South West Screen**, St Bartholomews Court, Lewins Mead, Bristol BS1 5BT, Tel: 0117 952 9977, Email: info@swscreen.co.uk, Website: www.swscreen.co.uk.
- **Screen East**, 1st Floor, 2 Millennium Plain, Norwich NR2 1TF, Tel: 0845 601 5670, Email: info@screeneast.co.uk, Website: www.screeneast.co.uk.
- **EM Media**, 35–37 St Mary's Gate, Nottingham NG1 1PU, Tel: 0115 934 9090, Email: info@em-media.org.uk, Website: www.em-media.org/.

If you're lucky enough to get on to one of the above schemes, you will probably be able to get your name put onto the SIF Trainee Network, run by the Skills Investment Fund (SIF), a database of trainee-level crew that production companies can browse through when they are looking to hire crew members. For more information, see www.sifnetwork.org.

VOCATIONAL QUALIFICATIONS
Before you start working ...
There are lots of media-related vocational qualifications you can get before you start working – GNVQs, NVQs or SVQs, City & Guilds, BTECs and Foundation degrees. To find out about all of them, speak to a career adviser (see Getting Advice on page 69). You can also look up courses on the UCAS database (www.ucas.ac.uk) or in the reference book, *British Vocational Qualifications* (Kogan Page). For information on City & Guilds courses, see www.city-and-guilds.co.uk. For information on BTECs, see www.edexcel.org.uk. For information on Foundation degrees, see www.foundationdegree.org.uk.

There are specific NVQs/SVQs that you'll need for some entry-level jobs and schemes. For example, the FT2 training scheme expects applicants to its Set Crafts Apprenticeship scheme, who go on to work in entry-level jobs, to already have the relevant CITB (Construction Industry Training Board) NVQ or SVQ at Level 2 in either Carpentry and Joinery, Painting and Decorating or Fibrous Plastering. For its Technical Training Scheme, people who want to apply to become Make-Up/Hair Assistants must already have achieved NVQs in Hairdressing and Beauty Therapy at Level 2.

For advice on which NVQs to do, speak to a skillsformedia adviser (08080 300 900) or to learndirect (0800 585 505). Also, see the NVQ website at www.dfes.gov.uk/nvq.

ON THE JOB
Once you're working, you can get **Skillset Professional Qualifications** (NVQs) – the 'gold standards' for the film, television, video and multimedia industry. These can't be done at college, only once you're working in the industry. Nor are they done by sitting exams – you are assessed on the job by an approved

'Skillset Standards were created by the industry for the industry. If we want to maintain our leading position in a global marketplace we should all be using them.'

David Puttnam, Producer of Midnight Express, Chariots of Fire, The Killing Fields *among others.*

assessor from one of Skillset's nine Assessment Centres around the country. Charges for being assessed vary, depending on how long it takes and whether you need to take any short courses to get the NVQ.

Each NVQ, which come at various levels, relates to a specific job, and is proof for future employers that you can do that job. More than 3,000 people already have them. The hope is that by making the Skillset NVQs a must-have, employers will have a much easier time recruiting people – they'll know exactly what candidates are capable of.

To find out more about the Skillset NVQs, see the Skillset website (www.skillset.org). Check out the Route Maps there – these list the Skillset NVQs and show you exactly what experience you need to achieve them. For advice on doing the Skillset NVQs, you could also speak to a skillsformedia adviser (Tel: 08080 300 900).

Modern Apprenticeships are for over-16s who want to train while working. There are two levels of Modern Apprenticeships: Foundation (FMA) and Advanced (AMA). Both lead to NVQs and other qualifications. There is a Modern Apprenticeship in broadcast, film, video and multimedia, which can be done while working in, for example, Post-production, Camera Assistance or Make-up.

To find out more, call 08000 150 600 or see the Modern Apprenticeships website (www.realworkrealpay.info). For information on Modern Apprenticeships in Scotland see www.modernapprenticeships.com/, in Wales www.beskilled.net and www.elwa.org.uk/, and in Northern Ireland www.delni.gov.uk.

FILM COURSES

Deciding whether or not to study film full-time is a big decision, especially if it's a postgraduate course you're paying for.

The pros are that you get a chance to totally immerse yourself in film-making and meet like-minded people to make short films with. The cons are that it can leave you up to your neck in debt and give you unreal expectations – a lot of people emerge from courses expecting to walk straight into good jobs. A lucky few do, but nearly everyone still has to start at the bottom, whether they've done a course or not.

If you do decide to do a course, it's important to make sure you choose the right one – one that will teach you genuinely useful skills, using proper industry-standard equipment.

Unfortunately, there is no single, gold standard accreditation system for courses, although Skillset is working on one. That means you're going to have to do lots of research. Remember, higher education is big business these days – course providers and their syllabuses are selling you their services, so make sure you ask some hard-hitting questions before applying.

Choosing the right course
- Read the prospectus carefully and check out the *Media Courses UK* guide (see below) for the low-down on the course. How much of it is practical? Study the syllabus. One sign of a good, vocational course, is that the syllabus is modelled around, or similar to, the Skillset Professional Qualifications – a good indication that it's gearing students up to do real jobs in the real world. To read more about the Skillset standards, see www.skillset.org.
- What kind of equipment do they have? Visit the facilities – does it look as if they have enough equipment for the number of students they take?
- Ask what industry links the course has. Do they help students find work experience? Where have previous students done placements?
- Ask what's happened to previous students – how many of them found jobs and doing what? Try and find former students to speak to about what was useful and useless about the course.
- What experience do the tutors have? Have any of them worked in film in recent years – if so, what on? Good courses often have tutors who've worked in the business, or are still working in it.

Finding out about film schools and courses
Whether you're looking for a full-time or part-time course, a long one or a short one, these are good places for doing research into the right course for you:

- **IDEAS**FACTORY (www.channel4.com/ideasfactory) has a course-finding service in its Training and Courses section. You can search or browse through hundreds of options.
- *Media Courses UK* by Lavinia Orton (BFI) – an annual and comprehensive guide to media courses, based on Skillset and the British Film Institute's database of courses. The annual *BFI Film &*

Television Handbook (BFI) also lists major undergraduate, postgraduate and other courses. Try your local library.

● Alternatively, you can search the Skillset/BFI database online for free, by place, institution or keyword, at www.bfi.org.uk/education/courses/mediacourses. Bear in mind that just because a course is listed there, it doesn't mean Skillset or the BFI are recommending it.

● skillsformedia (Tel: 08080 300 900; www.skillsformedia.com), LearnDirect (Tel: 0800 585 505; www.learndirect.co.uk) and Connexions www.connexions.gov.uk) can also advise on courses.

The UK Film Council gives financial support to various courses. The list is worth checking out, as it's a good indication of courses and training providers that the industry really rates. It's also a good indication of the skills gaps that the UK Film Council has identified – most of the courses it backs are for training script writers, development executives, business executives, producers and distributors. See the Training section on the UK Film Council website at www.filmcouncil.org.uk.

❝ MY EXPERIENCE

'The trouble with lots of courses is that they teach skills across the industry, so students leave with a very superficial knowledge. People come out of college and are really disappointed to find that out. Also, there's an oversupply of courses. I think the colleges are to blame – they take the money and promise careers that just aren't out there. If you do a course, get some experience on student films. I can't believe it when I meet people who have done media studies for three years without having worked on a student film. If you haven't got the gumption to do that, forget it, because you won't survive.'

Becky, Sound Recordist and Boom Operator

❞

Getting Funding
Tuition fees for film courses can be high, plus there are your living costs while you're studying. If it's your first, undergraduate degree you'll get

Online courses

There is a lot you can learn about film, without even having to leave your bedroom:

- **The Global Film School** (www.globalfilmschool.com) is an online university dedicated to filmmaking. It is run by the UCLA School of Theatre, Film and Television, in conjunction with the UK National Film & Television School and their Australian counterpart.
- **The BBC Training and Development** website (www.bbctraining.co.uk) has some of the courses it uses to train staff online – and for free. There are dozens to choose from, for example Pre-production, Post-production and Introduction to Video Production.
- **IDEAS**FACTORY has teamed up with Vision2Learn to offer **IDEAS**FACTORY visitors free online courses, mostly in career development skills. See the Training and Courses section on the **IDEAS**FACTORY website (www.channel4.com/ideasfactory).

some state funding, but for post-graduate or short courses there are, sadly, no big film training funds. Some courses have a few grants and bursaries, but it will probably be up to you to raise the cash. Here's where you can get some help:

- Career Development Loans – these are for between £300 and £8,000, for up to two years of training. Barclays, The Co-operative or The Royal Bank of Scotland lend the money, but the Department for Education and Skills pays the interest. To find out more, call the LearnDirect advice line (Tel: 0800 585 505) or see www.lifelonglearning.co.uk/cdl.
- For more information on getting financial help for training, get the Department for Education and Skills booklet *Money to Learn* (Tel: 0845 602 2260) or at www.lifelonglearning.co.uk/moneytolearn.
- There are charities you could write to, to ask for sponsorship. Try your local library for *The Directory of Grant Making Trusts*, the *Charities Digest* and the *Hollis Sponsorship and Donations Yearbook*.

DOING IT FOR YOURSELF

'Don't dream about being a filmmaker, you are a filmmaker.'

Robert Rodriguez, guerrilla filmmaker who made
El Mariachi *on a $7,000 budget and a borrowed 16mm camera*

'I think this is the liberation of filmmaking. I think such interesting things will come out of people's laptops now – I can't wait. I think it is a brilliant time to be making films.'

Mike Figgis, director of Internal Affairs, Leaving Las Vegas *and* Timecode, *which was shot in one take on digital cameras, talking about digital cameras and the Internet*

If you're desperate to make films, don't hang around dreaming about the day you get a job as a director. It could be a long, long way off. Start making films now. It's a cliché, but as any filmmaker will tell you, if you want to learn how to be a filmmaker, the best way is to make a film.

On the web

You can learn everything you need to know about film-making on the Internet. There are amazing resources out there for low-budget film-makers, as well as dozens of sites where you can hear about and talk to other filmmakers. Check these out, for starters:

- **Exposure** (www.exposure.co.uk) – everything you need to know to shoot your film, including an 'Eejit's Guide to Film-Making'.
- **Filmmaking.net** (www.filmmaking.net) – articles, resources and forums for new and independent film-makers, including a really useful FAQ section on film-making that advises on everything, from what to shoot your film on, to where to get royalty-free music.
- **Raindance** (www.raindance.co.uk) – Raindance runs courses, a film festival and this site, including a brilliant Indie Tips section.
- **Trigger St** (www.triggerstreet.com) – a web-based community for film-makers and scriptwriters, set up by Kevin Spacey, where anyone can upload their short film or script, and get it reviewed by peers.
- **IndieWIRE** (www.indiewire.com) – news about independent films, film-makers and festivals.
- **Shooting People** (www.shootingpeople.org) – this is the UK's largest online film community, with a membership of over 23,000. Pioneers of ambitious new attitudes and approaches to filmmaking.

There has never been a better time to do it yourself. Video and digital cameras have made filmmaking on a low budget a reality. They can be edited on Macs and PCs, and then marketed and distributed on the Internet.

There is also a thriving low-budget, 'guerrilla filmmaking' culture. Guerrilla filmmaking was pioneered by directors like Robert Rodriguez who made a hit film, *El Mariachi*, when he was 23. It cost $7,000 to make, money he raised by being a guinea pig for medical experiments.

Daniel Myrick and Eduardo Sanchez, two film students, shot *The Blair Witch Project* in eight days, on video, for $30,000. They used word of mouth and the Internet to market the film, creating a lot of hype before it came out and a massive box office hit when it was released.

'Your first film will probably turn out rubbish,' says Filmmaking.net, an excellent site for new and independent film-makers. 'And it is more than likely that the next couple will also look forward to being buried deep in the cupboard. Nonetheless, when you are starting out it is better to have two or three bad films behind you, than nothing at all. And you'll have learnt a hell of a lot at the same time.'

GUERRILLA FILMMAKING

- If you can, get hold of a copy of *The Guerrilla Filmmaker's Handbook* (Continuum) by Genevieve Jolliffe and Chris Jones. They write about their experiences making low-budget films in what has become a bible for low-budget film-makers.
- Check out Robert Rodriguez's book, *Rebel Without a Crew* (Faber and Faber). There is also *10 Minute Film School* by Robert Rodriguez, which you can read online at Exposure (www.exposure.co.uk).

MAKE THE MOST OF OPPORTUNITIES

Once you've started making films, there are masses of ways to get them noticed – at film festivals or in competitions. These are just a few of the opportunities open to new filmmakers. Also keep an eye on the Opportunities page in the Film and TV section of **IDEAS**FACTORY (www.channel4.com/ideasfactory) which has the latest news on festivals, short film competitions and new schemes.

Film festivals
- **Filmfestivals.com** (www.filmfestivals.com) has international festival listings, plus news of what's showing where.

- **Screen Daily** (www.screendaily.com) has an online Festival Calendar, with more than 500 festivals that can be searched by name, location or date.
- *The Ultimate Film Festival Survival Guide* by Chris Gore (Lone Eagle) has listings, as well as advice on how to work the festival scene and get yourself noticed.

Competitions and Funding

- **BBC Talent** – an annual competition, with categories for new film-makers, animators and pop promo directors. See www.bbc.co.uk/talent.
- **IDEAS**FACTORY Live – This is the offline incarnation of **IDEAS**FACTORY. It usually takes the form of a series of on-the-ground events, which evolves into a competition. **IDEAS**FACTORY Screenplay is an example of a recent competition: 200 would-be screenwriters in the West Midlands were taken through a series of workshops and masterclasses with renowned film practitioners, culminating in the production and broadcast on Channel 4 primetime of four of their short films. These competitions can be followed closely online at www.channel4.com/ideasfactory.
- **Vision Design Competition** – part of the selection process for BBC design trainee posts (see page 73). See www.bbc.co.uk/designvision/competition.
- **First Light** – UK Film Council funding and awards for short films by young film-makers (7–18 years). See www.firstlightmovies.com.
- **Digital Shorts** and **New Cinema Fund/FilmFour Lab** – various UK Film Council short film schemes. See www.filmcouncil.org.uk/shorts.
- **Mesh** – Channel 4's digital and interactive animation competition. See www.channel4.com/mesh.
- **Animate!** – Channel 4 and the Arts Council of England funding scheme for experimental animation. See www.animateonline.org.
- **Alt TV** – Channel 4's competition for factual film makers. See the Opportunities page in the Film and TV section of **IDEAS**FACTORY (www.channel4.com/ideasfactory) or contact: Independent Film & Video, Channel 4, 124 Horseferry Rd, London SW1P 2TX.
- **Nike Young Directors Awards** – Nike-sponsored short films competition, in association with Britshorts, a showcase site for UK and European shorts. See www.britshorts.com/nike.
- **Shooting People** – an online community for UK filmmakers (http://shootingpeople.org), has published an invaluable book on financing films, including information on getting awards and funds for shorts: *Get Your Film Funded: UK Film Finance Guide* by Caroline Hancock and Nic Wistreich (Shooting People Press).

GETTING A JOB

JOB HUNTING
Very few film jobs get advertised. There are rarely any formal recruitment procedures. This is a word-of-mouth, contacts-are-everything business. That means you're going to have to do a lot of research and learn how to sell yourself. You'll need a solid CV, a confident phone manner and plenty of determination.

Don't be put off. As a newcomer, the film job market can look alarmingly small and elitist. In many ways, it is. But it also surprisingly meritocratic – almost everyone in film started out at the bottom of the ladder and worked their way up. They'll expect you to do the same, no matter who you do or don't know, or what school or university you did or didn't go to.

Once you get the hang of how the job market works in film – where to look, who to speak to – you'll hopefully start getting some work. The key thing to remember about working in film is that one job leads to another. So it's vital to make the most of any work or work experience that comes your way, to shine while you can and get yourself noticed and remembered.

Where to look
The trade press and the Internet are your best bets when job-hunting, but check out local papers too for opportunities with regional companies. The national press is less likely to have ads for entry-level jobs, but keep an eye on Monday's Media section in the *Guardian* and its website (www.jobs.guardian.co.uk) – that's where major training schemes and opportunities get advertised, and there is also the occasional small ad for an entry-level job.

Trade press
- *Screen International* (www.screendaily.com)
- *Broadcast* (www.broadcastnow.co.uk)
- *AV – Audio Visual Magazine* (www.avmag.co.uk)
- *Campaign* (www.brandrepublic.com)
- *Media Week* (www.mediaweek.co.uk)
- *The Stage* (www.thestage.co.uk)
- *Ariel* – the BBC's in-house magazine, available by subscription or you can pick it up for free in any BBC building reception
- *Televisual*.

Online
These are websites where you can browse jobs ads or place your own ad:

- Shooting People (http://shootingpeople.org)
- Production Base (www.productionbase.co.uk)
- Mandy's International Film and Television Production Directory (www.mandy.com)
- The Knowledge Online (www.theknowledgeonline.com)
- Find a Job at the **IDEAS**FACTORY website: www.ideasfactory.com/careers/index.htm and click on 'Find a Job'.

How they got there
When Skillset did a survey of freelances working in the audio-visual industries, it asked them how they got their first break, about their 'original entry routes' into the industry. Here's what they said:

	Features (%)	Commercials (%)
Responded to job ad	14	12
Approached by employer	19	17
Contacted employer	26	31
Agency	6	3
Friend or relative	32	29
Word of mouth	9	12

	Corporate (%)	Animation (%)
Responded to job ad	26	12
Asked by an employer	12	6
Contacted employer	33	53
Agency	3	12
Friend or relative	22	24
Word of mouth	11	6

(Source: Skillset Freelance Survey, January 2002)

Jobs ops ... for people with disabilities
Four All is a website for TV producers, broadcasters, casting agents and others who want to employ people with disabilities in their programmes – either on screen or behind the camera. See www.fourall.org.

... and for ethnic minorities
The Cultural Diversity Network has an online database of black, Asian and other ethnic minority TV freelancers and staff. See www.channel4.com/diversity.

- UK Screen (www.ukscreen.com)
- BBC Jobs (www.bbc.co.uk/jobs)
- Grapevine Jobs (www.grapevinejobs.com)
- Film-tv.co.uk (www.film-tv.co.uk)
- Mad (www.mad.co.uk)
- Regional Film & Video (www.4rfv.co.uk)
- Film Cast (www.filmcast.org).

SENDING CVs
You're more likely to find work by sending out your CV to production companies and other potential employers, than answering a job ad that hundreds of other people have seen.

Just take a look at the How They Got There table on page 86 – it's proof that the majority of people working in film got their first break by contacting a company themselves.

Chances are your CV and letter will be opened, glanced at for about half a second and then put on a pile with dozens of others. It's still worth doing: when a production company has a sudden rush on, they'll go back to that pile of CVs, randomly pick a few up and call to see if the person is available to work – right now. That person could be you, so get your CV on those piles.

Nowadays it is also common to email your CV in. If you choose to do this, it may also be a good idea to make a follow-up phone call, as a busy potential employer may not have time to read your email as closely as you would like. Be aware that some employers may find unsolicited email approaches intrusive and hit the Delete button.

WHERE TO SEND CVs
- Find out who's making what when – and write to them asking about it. The only way to do this is to scour the trade press for small news briefs about who has got the green light to make a film and what projects are about to go into production. This is a basic, but crucial job-hunting technique and everyone starting out in film does it.
- Think about films, programmes and ads you love, find out who made them and send your CV to the company. The Internet is your best resource for this kind of research – just type the film name and 'crew', or 'credits', into Google (www.google.co.uk).
- These are the reference books where you'll find names, addresses and numbers. Most of them are too expensive to buy, but you'll find them in your local library:

The Knowledge (CMP Information)
BFI Film & Television Handbook (BFI)
The Guardian Media Guide (Atlantic Books)
The PACT Directory of Independent Producers (PACT)
Kays UK Production Manual (Kay Media)
Animation UK (A-UK Publishing).

DOs and DON'Ts
CVs

- Make your CV short – one side of A4 is enough.
- Do different CVs for different jobs – they need to be tailored for different jobs and companies.
- Go backwards – list your most recent jobs or education first.
- There are no rules for laying out CVs, but in general it's best to highlight your experience before your education.
- Consider including a 'personal statement' or 'personal profile' at the top – a couple of lines summing up who you are and what skills and experience you have. For example: 'A Media Studies graduate, trained in camera work, with experience working as a Clapper Loader on professional and student films.'
- It's nearly always better to send a sound, solid, confident CV than a supposedly zany, wacky one – unless you have a truly, mind-blowingly original idea or an astoundingly witty one. Most people reading CVs have seen all the gimmicks before – bright-coloured paper, flattering photos, sweets. They won't be impressed. They want people who can do jobs, not jokers.

The perfect CV

No, there isn't really any such thing as the perfect CV. But to help you write a CV perfect for you, here's how skillsformedia suggest people lay out their CVs:

Your name
Job title
Contact details
Personal profile
Key skills
Experience
Training
Personal details – age, interests, nationality, driving licence

(Source: skillsformedia at www.skillsformedia.com)

- Get some advice. skillsformedia (Tel: 08080 300 900, Website: www.skillsformedia.com) can give you help brushing up your CV.
- Channel 4's **IDEAS**FACTORY website also has a Plan Your CV section with useful advice and hints on creating a CV with impact. Go to www.ideasfactory.com/careers, then click on 'Knowledge', and you will find a helpful CV-making tool.

Covering letters

- Write a short, one-page covering letter. Make sure it's addressed to the right person – call beforehand to check exactly who you should send it to. Spell their name, and everything else in the CV and letter, correctly.
- The letter should have a simple format – say (briefly) why you're writing, who you are and what you've done, why you are writing to them in particular and that you'll hope they'll be in touch, or could you meet?
- Make it clear in the letter what kind of work you're interested in. It drives people crazy when they get 'I'm-desperate-to-work-in-film, I'll-do-anything' letters. So say (roughly) what kind of job it is that you're after, and in what department.

Calls

- Don't call to say you're sending your CV – they won't care.
- Do call to say you've sent it – make a couple of follow-up calls, one soon after you sent the CV, another later.
- On the phone, ask when would be a good time to call back – are they likely to be looking for staff in a few weeks or a few months?

> **"** INSIDER TIP
>
> 'Dates are really important. When you call somewhere, or speak to anyone, try and get some dates out of them – even a rough idea of when they're going into production. Also, call the big production bases, like Goldcrest, where production companies rent offices when they're in production. Ask reception which companies are there at the moment, then call them.'
>
> *Laura, Production Assistant*
>
> **"**

- Try to get chatting with the person on the other end, but also try to sound like you're only going to take 30 seconds of their time. These people get dozens of calls a week, and their hearts sink when the person calling doesn't get to the point fast. So be quick.

INTERVIEWS

- Feel confident. Make sure you're well prepared and have done your research. Then you can really *be* confident. If you've been asked in for an interview, they obviously think that, on paper at least, you're made of the right stuff. People don't waste time interviewing people they don't think have the right skills, experience or outlook.
- Research the company and maybe even the person interviewing you – what kind of work they do, what projects they have worked on and what they have got coming up. Check out their website and look them up in film reference books (see Where to Send CVs, on page 87).
- First impressions matter. Smile, stand up straight. Unless you're going for a job on the business side of film, you probably don't need to wear a suit. In fact, for some jobs it could work against you. Ask someone who works in that field what you should wear.
- Shake hands with whoever's interviewing you. When someone asks you a question, look them in the eye when you're answering, but make sure not to ignore anyone else present too. If you feel nervous and twitchy, put your hands in your lap and keep them there.
- You'll probably be asked if you have any questions, so prepare some beforehand. If you don't have any, it can look like you're not interested.

EXERCISES TO GET YOUR HEAD IN GEAR

Before you write all those CVs and letters, and before you go off to an interview, or even just for an informal chat with someone, it helps to gather some of your thoughts about why it is you want to work in the industry or in a particular job. These exercises will help get you in the right frame of

On the web

IDEASFACTORY has an Ideasbank full of exercises designed to get your creative juices flowing. Check them out in the Knowledge in the Film and TV area at www.channel4.com/ideasfactory.

mind for talking about film, expressing your views and generally showing enthusiasm.

- Make a list of your top ten favourite films, TV shows, commercials or animation work – and think about why you love them so much and how you'd argue their case.
- What film, TV show, commercial or animation has impressed you most in the past year? Think about it in relation to the job you want to do. So, for example, if you want to work in lighting, think of a production with stunning lighting. Maybe find out who made it and what techniques they used.

JARGON BUSTER

Storyboard
A storyboard is a visual plan of the film – a series of illustrations, photos, sketches and captions showing, shot by shot, how a scene is going to be captured on camera. They can look a bit like comic strips.

- Make a showreel, or put together a portfolio of photos, drawings, designs, graphics or sound you've recorded, or part of a storyboard. If you want to write, write a script for a short. Not only can you take these with you to interviews, but the process of making or preparing them will teach you about film-making.
- Start keeping a creative notebook. Record your ideas in it, notes about films or commercials you've seen, and stuff it with striking images and

Sight & Sound top ten films

Back in 1952 *Sight & Sound* magazine polled the world's leading film critics to create a list of the best films of all time. The magazine now does it again every ten years. Here's what the critics said in 2002:

1. Citizen Kane
2. Vertigo
3. La Règle du jeu
4. The Godfather and The Godfather (Part II)
5. Tokyo Story
6. 2001: A Space Odyssey
7. Battleship Potemkin
8. Sunrise
9. 8½
10. Singin' In the Rain

(*Source: Sight & Sound* at www.bfi.org.uk/sightandsound)

articles you've come across – postcards, pictures and graphics ripped out of magazines.

BOOST YOUR CONFIDENCE

Faced with a blank page, it's easy to feel you don't have any skills or experience worth mentioning in a CV. You do – you just need to take time to identify them, and to learn the art of putting the right spin on achievements that at first glance might seem run-of-the-mill. You will find you are listing your 'transferable skills'. These are skills that you can apply in many different jobs and situations - for example IT skills or the ability to communicate well, which are valuable in any work situation.Have a think about these:

- What IT skills do you have? List them. Skills that may seem bog standard to you, won't necessarily seem so to others – you'd be stunned how many people still don't know how to use the Internet. If you know how, say so.
- What have you organised in the past? Are there any events, trips, parties you've organised that you can point to, to show off your research and organisational skills?
- What jobs have you done, including Saturday and holiday jobs? Think of anything you've done before where you've had to work in a team, any job where you've had to sell or promote something, or anything you've done where you've been given a level of responsibility.
- Finally, what do you know about? What are you into? Do you know more than anyone else you know about extreme climbing, obscure Elizabethan plays or bloggers? If so, say you do – you never know, they might need someone who knows about those worlds.

WORK EXPERIENCE

You're much more likely to get a job, or get on a training scheme, if you've got some work experience. It shows you're committed to a career in film and know something about the business, rather than just vaguely wanting to 'work in film'. Not only that, work experience can lead to real work, or at least to making some important first contacts.

It also gives you a chance to see whether or not the film world is for you. After one week of long hours in a cramped office, being totally ignored or rudely ordered around, you may decide it's not for you.

Finding work experience is not always easy. Production companies get hundreds of requests a year. To stand a chance, you need to treat looking for work experience like job-hunting. That means researching which companies to approach and then sending well-written, easy-to-read CVs and covering letters.

That said, just because there is fierce competition to find work experience, it doesn't mean you should allow yourself to be exploited. Lots of people have work experience horror stories to tell, mostly about working for months on end, unpaid. A few years ago one London production company was *charging* people for the privilege of doing work experience.

PACT has a work experience code of practice for production companies offering placements. It says that no one should work unpaid for more than four weeks and that travel and other expenses should be covered. After four weeks, the role should turn into a paid training post. It also says there should be equal opportunities for work experience candidates.

Given the often casual, haphazard nature of the film business, it's unlikely you'll find many companies adhering to these guidelines – and it's very hard to say 'No' to a long stint of hands-on experience, even if it's unpaid. So set yourself a limit – decide how long you want, or can afford, to work unpaid, and stick to it.

If you're doing well in a placement and they want you to stay on, tell them you'd love to, but you've got a time limit on unpaid work, and simply can't afford to do more without being paid. If they need you, they'll start paying.

❝ INSIDER TIP

'Work experience is valuable and all very good, but if you're doing a proper job you should get paid. I have worked for free, and everybody does stints on low-budget productions directed or produced by friends and students, and that's fine. But I've also been interviewed for jobs at companies with 20 plus staff, all getting paid except the Runner. Don't do it. If one person gets a wage, everybody should get a wage.'

Josh, Runner

❞

Finding work experience

- Use the Internet to check whether companies have work experience schemes. It will save you a lot of letter-writing time if you find out first that they *don't* take people on placements.
- When writing letters or calling to ask for work experience, it may help to be specific – say what kind of experience you're after, in the production office or with the camera crew, rather than just that you want experience 'in film'.
- As well as writing to companies, write to individuals. If you want to work in an Art Department, find out the name of a Production Designer on a film you admired and write to them, saying you like their work, and ask if there is any chance of shadowing them for a few days.
- The BBC website lets you search for placements online, in specific areas – cameras, design or finance, for example. See the Work Experience page at BBC Jobs (www.bbc.co.uk/jobs/workexperience_hub.shtml).
- Channel 4 offers a limited number of short-term work experience placements to people with a strong desire to work in the media. These positions are in high demand, and successful applicants need to demonstrate a keen desire to work at the channel. You can send your CV and cover letter to: HR Work Experience, Channel 4, 124 Horseferry Road, London SW1P 2TX.
- Get some work experience at a film school, working on student films. Some, like the National Film and Television School, offer placements. For more information, contact the NFTS (Tel: 01494 671 234, Website: www.nftsfilm-tv.ac.uk).

❝ INSIDER TIP

'If you can, try and get some work on short films, maybe student ones. You get great hands-on experience, a bit of responsibility and people show you how to do things. On bigger productions, everyone's too busy to do that. But on short films, people talk to each other.'

Karen, Runner

NETWORKING

Networking ... What does it mean? It sounds so formal, so phoney. Don't worry – networking just means talking to people, thinking of anyone you know who knows anything about film, and then asking them for any advice or contacts they have. That's all. Make the most of all the contacts you have. Think about family, family friends, teachers, etc. and any connections they may have with the industry. On reflection, it could turn out to be quite an extensive network of useful contacts. It's a numbers game really - don't underestimate the value of this kind of networking.

The Internet is a great place to make new contacts, with loads of buzzing film forums where people swap ideas, views and advice. Try these:

- **IDEAS**FACTORY (www.channel4.com/ideas factory)
- Exposure (www.exposure.co.uk)
- Shooting People (http://shootingpeople.org)

Networking – or whatever you want to call it – is essential in the film business. Skillset's Freelance Survey in 2002 found more than a third of people got their first break in features through a friend or relative. Contacts aren't just important for your first job – making friends with people on jobs, and keeping in touch with them afterwards, is how most people go on getting jobs in film.

- Think of anyone you know you works in film, or used to. If you don't know anyone, ask friends if they do, and maybe ask them to call to say you're going to be in touch. If you're feeling brave, you could contact people you have no connection with, but who might be able to give you some advice – look up some names in the film reference books or find them in film credits. If you're feeling shy, contact people by email.
- If you are given someone's name and number, make sure you know who they are and what they do before you call. Introduce yourself, explain that 'so and so' suggested you give them a call and ask if they've got time for a brief chat on the phone at some point, or maybe even to meet for 15 minutes.
- If they say 'Yes', you've got yourself an 'informational interview'. The idea is to get as much information about a company, project, job or career as you can. You're basically asking them for advice on how to get ahead – the low-down on what steps you should be taking.
- If you're speaking to someone who might be in a position to offer you work, it's usually better to say you just want a 'chat', rather than saying you want a job. At the end, ask if it's OK to send your CV.

Be an extra

You could try getting work as an extra. Besides its potential to be fun, it can also be useful experience, giving you a valuable insight into the mechanics of filmmaking and what happens on set. The Film Artists' Association says pay should be about £70 a day with £25 more for a 'walk-on' part. It can be more. Register with as many agencies as you can. See the UK Screen website (www.ukscreen.com/agent) for a list. Men between 25 and 40 are, it is said, the most in demand – to be policemen, soldiers and football fans. People who are over 18, but look younger, are also popular.

- Ask everyone you speak to who else you should speak to – that's how you build a network of contacts. Always thank them profusely for sparing the time to talk – and if anyone ever asks you for help in future, return the favour.
- Finally, if you still feel anxious about the thought of asking people for help, remember that on the whole, people *love* being asked for advice. It's very flattering, and a great chance to talk about themselves.

SURVIVING FINANCIALLY

One of the hardest things about getting started in film is the money. You don't get paid for work experience, and even when you do get a job, it is usually short-term and the pay is, well, not exactly what you'd get in the City. Harder still, most of the work is in London, not a cheap city when it comes to accommodation and getting about.

A lot of people drop out of film after a few years, or even months. Often, money is the deciding factor. So if you're going to make it through those tough first years, you're going to have to be shrewd about cash. Temping is often the best solution – it means you can work on days when you haven't got a film job, but you're still available for film work if someone calls you up at the last minute. You might even be able to find temp work within the film world, doing filing for a production company or being a receptionist at a facilities house.

'The film industry has its ups and downs but if you're determined and hard-working, you'll be able to ride that roller-coaster. The film business needs a new generation of people with talent and specialist skills – and you could be one of them.'

7. GOING FOR IT
commit to your career

Now you know about what it's like to work in film, and how people get into it, take some time to think seriously about whether this is the career for you.

Getting training, and your first few breaks, is hard, and even when you're 'in', it goes on being hard. The freelance life is not for everyone. Nor is hanging around on a freezing cold location for 16 hours a day, six days a week. So think carefully about whether you've got the character and commitment to embark on what could be some long hours, on low pay, on a long road to the top.

It may be that film is almost, but not quite right for you. If so, maybe you should consider a career in television or radio? There are more jobs and more stability in both, but they are equally rewarding. Check out *Creative Careers: Television* and *Creative Careers: Radio* (Trotman).

If you started reading this book knowing that you wanted to work in film and, now you've got to the end, you still want to work in film – go for it.

The film industry has its ups and downs, and so does everyone working in it, but if you're determined and hard-working, you'll be able to ride that roller-coaster. In September 2003 the UK Film Council and Skillset launched a groundbreaking £10 million-a-year package of measures, for at least five years, geared towards attracting Britain's brightest and best into a career in the film industry. Check out the details of this new initiative at www.ukfilmcouncil.org. This £50 million aims to produce the next generation of UK film talent. The film business needs people with talent and specialist skills – and you could be part of the new generation.

8. FIND OUT MORE

Have a look over the On the Web boxes that have appeared throughout this book for a reminder of how much help and guidance you can find on the Internet.

USEFUL ORGANISATIONS

GENERAL
British Film Institute
21 Stephen Street
London W1T 1LN
Tel: 020 7255 1444
Website: www.bfi.org.uk

PACT – Producers Alliance for Cinema and Television
45 Mortimer Street
London W1W 8HJ
Tel: 020 7331 6000
Website: www.pact.co.uk

Skillset and **Skillsformedia**
Prospect House
80–110 New Oxford Street
London WC1A 1HB
Tel: 020 7520 5757
Websites: www.skillset.org and www.skillsformedia.com

UK Film Council
10 Little Portland Street
London W1W 7JG
Tel: 020 7861 7861
Website: www.filmcouncil.org.uk

GUILDS AND TRADE ASSOCIATIONS
Advertising Producers' Association
26 Noel Street
London W1F 8GT
Tel: 020 7434 2651
Website: www.a-p-a.net

British Film Designers Guild
78 Loudoun Road
London NW8 0NA
Tel: 020 7722 0754
Website: www.filmdesigners.co.uk

British Society of Cinematographers
PO Box 2587
Winsor Road
Gerrards Cross
Bucks SL9 7WZ
Tel: 01753 888 052
Website: www.bscine.com

Casting Directors Guild
PO Box 34403
London W6 0YG
Tel: 020 8741 1951
Website: http://castingdirectorsguild.co.uk/

Directors Guild of Great Britain
Acorn House
314–320 Gray's Inn Road

London WC1X 8DP
Tel: 020 7278 4343
Website: www.dggb.co.uk

Film Distributors Association
22 Golden Square
London W1F 9JW
Tel: 020 7437 4383
Website:www.launchingfilms.co.uk

Guild of British Camera Technicians
GBCT, c/o Panavision UK
Metropolitan Centre
Bristol Road
Greenford
Middlesex UB6 8GD
Tel: 020 8813 1999
Website: www.gbct.org

Guild of British Film Editors
72 Pembroke Road
London W8 6NX
Tel: 020 7602 8319

Guild of Location Managers
20 Euston Centre
Regent's Place
London NW1 3JH
Tel: 020 7387 8787
Website: www.golm.org.uk

Music Video Producers Association
26 Noel Street
London W1F 8GT
Tel: 020 7434 2651
Website: www.mvpa.co.uk

New Producers Alliance
9 Bourlet Close
London W1W 7BP
Tel: 020 7580 2480
Website: www.npa.org.uk

Production Guild of Great Britain
Pinewood Studios
Pinewood Road
Iver Heath
Bucks SL0 0NH
Tel: 01753 651 767
Website: www.productionguild.com

Production Managers Association
Ealing Studios
Ealing Green
London W5 5EP
Tel: 020 8758 8699
Website: www.pma.org.uk

Association of Professional Recording Services
PO Box 22
Totnes
Devon TQ9 7YZ
Tel: 01803 868 600
Website: www.aprs.co.uk

Women in Film and Television
6 Langley Street
London WC2H 9JA
Tel: 020 7240 4875
Website: www.wftv.org.uk

Writers' Guild of Great Britain
15 Britannia Street
London WC1X 9JN
Tel: 020 7833 0777
Website: www.writersguild.org.uk

UNIONS
BECTU – Broadcasting, Entertainment, Cinematograph and Theatre Union
373–377 Clapham Road
London SW9 9BT
Tel: 020 7346 0900
Website: www.bectu.org.uk

AMICUS – Amalgamated Engineering and Electrical Union
Hayes Court
West Common Road
Hayes
Bromley
Kent BR2 7AU
Tel: 020 8462 7755
Website: www.aeeu.org.uk

USEFUL BOOKS

BFI Film & Television Handbook, edited by Eddie Dyja (BFI)
A Career Handbook for TV, Radio, Film, Video & Interactive Media by
    Shiona Llewellyn and Sue Walker (Skillset, A&C Black)
The Knowledge (CMP Information)
The PACT Directory (PACT)
The Guerrilla Film-maker's Handbook by Chris Jones and Genevieve
    Jolliffe (Continuum)
*Rebel Without a Crew: How a 23-year-old Film-maker with $7,000 Became
    a Hollywood Player* by Robert Rodriguez (Faber and Faber)
Breaking into Film by Kenna Mchugh (Vacation Work, US)
Story: Substance, Structure, Style, and the Principles of Screenwriting by
    Robert McKee (HarperCollins)
The Definitive Guide to Screenwriting by Syd Field (Ebury)
Get Your Film Funded: UK Film Finance Guide by Caroline Hancock and Nic
    Wistreich (Shooting People Press)

TROTMAN BOOKS ON GETTING INTO AND WORKING IN THE MEDIA

Creative Careers: Television by Milly Jenkins
Creative Careers: Radio by Tania Shillam
Q & A: Radio, Television & Film A Questions & Answers Careers Book
Getting into the Media by Emma Caprez